DREAMS AND VISIONS

The Life and Influence of JayQuan Taylor

BY EVANGELIST: MARY A LUCAS

Copyright © 2014 by Evangelist: Mary A Lucas

Dreams and Visions
The Life and Influence of JayQuan Taylor
by Evangelist: Mary A Lucas

Printed in the United States of America

ISBN 9781498414265

All rights reserved solely by the author. The author guarantees all contents are original and do not infringe upon the legal rights of any other person or work. No part of this book may be reproduced in any form without the permission of the author. The views expressed in this book are not necessarily those of the publisher.

Scripture.quotations taken from the King James Version (KJV) – *public domain.*

www.xulonpress.com

TABLE OF CONTENTS

CHAPTER I 5

CHPATER II 22

CHAPTER III 54

CHAPTER I

This story begins like a lot of other story but the only difference is a young man name JayQuan. JayQuan and his mother were leaving Oklahoma because of the hurricane that swept their home and everything they had away. JayQuan's mother Juanita had buried their life saving in the backyard in a jar of preserves; you know like peaches and pears and other fruit, there were no preserves in the jar but money was there instead, she was looking very hard for the area that she buried it. There was rubble all around the area and she couldn't tell just by looking at the area it was a disaster but just as she thought she looked up and prayed to God Lord please let me find my jar. JayQuan didn't know what she was saying he said mom what is it, she said nothing son God just told me what I need to know and where I need to go, so she moved to her right about a foot over where she thought it was and said help me Quan she started digging and he said mom what are we doing this for everything is gone but there it was the jar. Now she said lets go, go where come with me.

JayQuan and his mother ended up in a small town outside of Chicago and they lived like squatters, she had to be careful about how she spent their money, they also met a lady and her son which is about the age of JayQuan they are about 18 years old. They all meet up together and they lived off the land. One day JayQuan and his new friend Carl went into town.

Now JayQuan mother said I don't want you going into town it is a dangerous place to be; JayQuan said to his mother mom I know you don't want me caught up in some kind trouble I will not get mixed up in drugs, drinking, or any other bad habits trust me I love you; JayQuan's mother said I love you also be careful and come home soon. Now JayQuan and Carl (his new friend) went into town. Chicago is a very big town Carl said and JayQuan said it is man I don't know if I've ever been in a town quit as big, lots of cars going by and fire trucks and also Big Riggs (Trucks) just as they were looking around they went in to a movie theater. When they came out of the theater they were laughing and remembering the parts of the story they had saw in the movie. So they said man let's try and come to see another movie next week OK (man would you look at that), just as JayQuan was about to answer him is eyes caught on to this young lady walking across the street, and Carl saw her too, Carl said wait man you can't go over there to her because she belongs to a pimp name Jay Dog and before he could get it out of his mouth JayQuan was gone he was across the street introducing himself to the young lady.

Hello my name is JayQuan what is your name she said Robin he said that is a beautiful name she said thank you, but she was also looking around for JayDog and then she said I'm going home excuse me and JayQuan said how about I walk you home she said No that's not necessary. JayQuan said oh it's no trouble, I will see you home, and it's

Chapter I

not safe for a young beautiful lady such as yourself to walk home alone; she could not and didn't want to stop him. Robins said when they got to her house thank you I have never seen a nice and polite young man as yourself before. I'm new in town but I would like to get to know you better, she said I don't think you would like my company. It's quite obvious that you are new in town if you still want to see me after the buzz around town gets to you I will see you. OH Yeah! JayQuan was so excited so when he caught up with Carl; JayQuan said hey, wait up man. Carl started tell him man you don't want to get involve with that girl man she is the town prostitute. JayQuan said man don't talk about her that way, she will one day be my wife! Carl said man you are crazy her boyfriend is a cat name JayDog and he will chew you up and spit you out, that's his money man don't you hear me, JayQuan was in a daze, oh yeah man I hear you. JayQuan was so taken with Robin he had made up in his mind that she would be his wife. So they went home and JayQuan's Mother notice something different about her son, she said how was the movie boys; and Carl said fine Mrs. Taylor and JayQuan said it was the most beautiful thing I have ever seen in my life, I love you and kissed her. She said what kind of movie was it that makes you act this way; he said life mom life, it goes on no matter what happen in Oklahoma.

JayQuan's Mother said Carl, is everything's alright and he said ah yes mame he's alright!

All night JayQuan dreamed about Robin. The next morning JayQuan greeted his mother with a kiss and she said thank you what was that for and he said because you are so beautiful and you started your life over again after what has happen to us and you never complain about not having things in life, but one day mom I will buy you everything that you need, a big fine house to live in and a car for you to drive it's going to be alright. She looked at her son with surprise in her eyes, ok son whatever you say! Now come and eat something I'm not hungry mom, now she is really worried, she knows something is up!

JayQuan said I'll see you later mom and she said are you and Carl going to see another movie so soon. He said no mom I'm just going for a walk, she said ok but be, he said I know be careful! She said there are a lot of bad things in this world that you don't know about JayQuan, so please be careful, I will mom, he shouted. JayQuan was on his way to see Robin she was looking out of her window when she saw JayQuan and she said what are you doing here didn't you hear what people are saying about me, he said no one knows better than I, that you don't want to do what you are doing I'm here to restore you. I am going to be the best friend you have ever had in your life starting now get dress and meet me downstairs, come on now I'm waiting. She could not believe that she was going but she never had a friend before that cared about her that's how she got involve with Jay Dog, he cruises the bus depot for teens that have run away from home. Robin was 15 when he got her to trust him, and so she is not the only young girl there in the Big House, there are plenty young ladies in their teens that work with Robin, and she is the oldest, she is 20 years old. JayDog gets the young ladies that run away from home and tells them that he is there friend and he will take good care of them so he gives them a place to sleep and then he buys them clothes and food and then they belong to him, now they are trapped, because they can't pay him back for everything that he bought. It's called human trafficking; America needs to wake up to these Predator's.

Chapter I

Now Robin is ready but she is looking behind her to see if JayDog is around; because she knows if he catches her, he will beat her or something worse, kill her. She is the one who is in charge of the other girls, she is suppose to kept them inline. Now they are at the movies and they are having a good time Robin has never had a good time before. JayQuan is telling her about the movie which is a love story of course. They are laughing and talking and eating popcorn and laughing about the movie and other things in life that Robin never experience, little things like going to a movie and having fun and shopping just for fun going to school, she dropped out at a early age. All though she is 20 and JayQuan is 18 she is like a little girl who has awaken at Christmas and getting the gift she always wanted. Now without knowing she is falling in love with JayQuan because he treats her like a lady and he has not touch her physically at all not even to kiss her, he is a gentleman, she never knew a gentleman in her life. Robin looks at JayQuan and she starts to cry and he said if this picture is going to make you cry I will take you to another theater; She said no it's not that, I love being here with you, and he said good I'm glad, so are you ready to go, she said I wish this moment would last forever! JayQuan said I can make that happen! Let's go and I will see you tomorrow, she said (under her breath) don't leave me JayQuan, he said what is it; she said nothing I've had a wonderful time today and I just wanted it to last, I'll see you tomorrow, you are not going to get rid of me that easy, don't worry you will see me tomorrow be ready ok, yes I'll be ready! Now JayQuan knows he is falling head over hill with Robin!

Now JayQuan's mother is in town and she see's JayQuan with Robin and she is not happy to say the least. Quan, his mother yells, why are you here with her she is my friend I met the other day so that's why you all of a sudden very loving with God's world right! Mom you don't know but I'm going to marry her one day. Oh you are (are you,) yes I am. Do you know what people are saying about this girl mother I love her so don't say anything bad about my future wife, let's go home now, I'm starving what did you cook, some of my favorite foods I bet, she starts to laughing and said boy you are something else, and JayQuan said I know mother I know but you love me anyway!

So now they are walking home. So after they get home, after JayQuan eat. While JayQuan is sleeping his mother takes it upon herself to go and talk to Robin. So you are JayQuan's Mother how nice to meet you, I'm sorry I can't say the same, I just came to tell you to stay away from my son. You can't possibly care for him; Mrs. Juanita says, I am telling you to stay away from my son he is not like any other man you have been with, Ma'am I know that, he is not like any man in this world he's polite, he's thoughtful, gentle, and kind. He's a perfect gentleman when I'm with him. I never had that before I know you don't approve of me but I love your son! My son is saved he loves God and you will not corrupt him, you don't know what love is how can you say you love him, now I've said all I came to say goodbye! While Ms. Juanita was talking to Robin she stayed a little longer than she had expected to, while she was leaving JayQuan was coming around the corner and saw his mother, mom what are you doing here. Quan I just wanted, I hope you didn't do what I think you did, Quan I love you I don't want you to make a big mistake, mom you made the mistake, Quan wait! Robin, come down her please, I can't see you any more, Robin I love you get dress we are going to get married. What did you say, come on don't you want to marry me, OH Yes JayQuan yes; I'm coming wait for me! They left town that morning and they got married. Robin was so happy and

Chapter I

so was JayQuan. Now I know you're saying what happen to Jay Dog and why he didn't stop the wedding? That's a very good question, Jay Dog has just heard about Robin leaving he was on his way there to find out why she has not been working like she is suppose to, entertaining other men. Now he is just livid! He is looking all over town for her and JayQuan he knows his name now, but they left town to live somewhere else, miles and miles away.

It's been years now JayQuan and Robin are expecting their first child. They are so happy, Robin is now a Preacher she has her own church she minister to prostitutes and junkies and gang members she has a church that God put together and she preaches and JayQuan preaches there also they take turns they love the community that they live in, and they try and help in any way that they can they live in the back of the church beautiful little church.

One Day Carl saw JayQuan and he called his name (Quan) and he said I'm so sorry man; I didn't know you was that serious about her, you mean Robin my wife; yes I thought that you could not forgive me. I wasn't a very good friend to you. Don't worry I forgive you, you didn't know we're still friends, here is my number call me sometimes and we can talk or you can come to the church and visit. Ok man thanks. JayQuan went home and Robin is expecting in a couple of months. He cooks for her; he makes her a warm bath every night.

This particular night he runs water in the tub for Robin and puts rose pedals in her water and she says what am I going to do with you and he said (keep me of course), so she says you bet I will. He tells her I will never leave you I will always be by your side forever! The world has been condition to say behind every great man is a great woman, but I say beside every great man is a greater women with wisdom and power! He kisses her then the phone rings its Carl he wants to see JayQuan and so he ask where are you, he said I am at the club, JayQuan said what club he said the one I've been going to after you left, Charlottes Club (regular hang out place for young people) you don't know it but it is and JayQuan is saying ok I can find it I'll be there soon. Robin said Honey where are you going this late, he said I'll be back soon before you can miss me. I'm going to see Carl he is acting very strange lately, ok but be careful I will, love you, love you back!

Now JayQuan comes in the door of Charlottes Club and see's Carl get a drink and JayQuan said man you should not be here and you should not be drinking, I know man I just can't forgive myself the way I acted before you left me behind, what are you talking about; man we were good friend we hung out together and almost live together I miss you Quan, hay man it's alright I'm just married now and I am a Pastor of a church and my wife is co-pastor and we are doing a lot for the community, come by we need to see you in the church ok Carl said! Then the phone rang, honey where are you I'm about to get out of the tub and get in the bed, I'm on my way, I'm worried, don't worry, you better get out of that tub before you spout gills like a fish you've been in there awhile I know I'm getting out now, love you, love you back.

Just then the door open and Jay Dog came in and he saw Carl and JayQuan he pulled out his gun and started shooting and they scrambled on the floor and the lights were shoot out no one could see and then the back door open you see people scrambling to get out down went people who were shoot and then you here Robin on the phone screaming JayQuan's name and the people are screaming she could not hang up the phone she just here a lot of screaming and shoots being fire; now she is in labor she has to hang up the phone to call 911 emergency I'm in labor my baby is coming. Just then the paramedics come to the door and can't get in; so they kick the door down, and she is having the baby in the tub, and the baby comes out. The paramedics trying to take the baby and give him mouth to mouth because he is not breathing. One of the paramedics see that she is not breathing he said I got to get her out of the tub she is not breathing we are losing her fast, it's like she doesn't want to live, Robin (my husband is gone and my baby is gone I have nothing to live for).

So the door opens and JayQuan comes in and he said you do have something to live for see our son he took the baby and the baby is breathing now very well and he kissed Robin she said I thought that you were, he said I'm here I said you will never get rid of me that easy I love you, I will never leave your side you must live and raised our son JayLin, she said that's beautiful JayLin ok JayLin it is, so the paramedics had called for a helicopter and it came and they all went to the hospital and JayQuan gave his son to the nurse and they rushed Robin in to the operating room. Now it is getting very tense and then while everyone Carl and his mother is down the hall Carl got shoot in the arms when JayQuan pushed him out of the way, while Jay Dog was shooting. They came to see Robin, but she couldn't see anyone just yet.

The police came to the hospital to talk to Robin and the doctors said she needs her rest now, she cannot talk just yet. The paramedics were still there and they said why don't you talk to her husband he rode with us in the helicopter. The detective said what did you just say? The doctor said you should talk to her husband they brought her in with him and the paramedics.

The detective said, why do you think I want to talk to her, her husband was killed this evening at a club called Charlotte's. They looked at the detective like he was crazy, they said you are very much mistaking and Carl said no he isn't I was with him when he died. The doctor, then who is that man in the waiting room? They ran in to see him and he was not there the nurse said he gave me the baby and went into the waiting room. We can't explain but he was here! JayQuan's mother was at the morgue identifying her son's body!

Now JayQuan saved Carl from the fatal bullet, which hit him, and he also saved his wife in more ways than one; and Carl and his Mother (Carl's mom) got saved at Robin's church and Robin still remain the preacher, because she loved God as much as JayQuan did. She knew that was what JayQuan would have wanted, and he taught her how to love God. Ms. Juanita Taylor raised her grandson JayLin along with Robin. Now Jay Dog got what he deserved, doing twenty years to life behind bars, but sometimes God comes to the jail house to save a person if he/she repents; thee other young girls that JayDog had in his stable (The Big House) also begin coming to Robin's church, as they wanted to be saved as well. JayQuan still lives!!!

This young man didn't live his life like every other young man; JayQuan's mother was a very good influence on him, because, I guess, his father wasn't around to teach him, so his mother took over to teach him the ways of God. I would say that she did a very good job. Some of us (mothers, that is) don't think of teaching the word of God to our children; that's not good. I made the same mistake with my oldest child; I didn't talk enough about God the father and Jesus, the Son of God, and the Holy Spirit of God; the three being God all by Himself!!! The Word of God says, that we need, to teach our children day and night about the word.

This is the end of chapter 1; the next chapter is another one of my dreams and visions God gave to me. Let me just tell you a few things, before I get to the next chapter.

A lot of us call ourselves Christians and don't even know the meaning of being a Christian. First of all, being called a Christian is a privilege, not a burden. Some people walk around looking like there is something wrong all the time. Now I know that being a Christian doesn't mean that there will not be bad times in our lives, but we don't have to look like the world is coming to an end, just because something didn't turn out the way we wanted it.

God will always give us away out of anything, if we are called according to His will. Nothing will happen, unless it is in the will of God. If we are His children He will keep us from falling, if we let Him.

Bad things happen to good and bad people: Good things happen to Good and bad people. God causes it to rain on the just and the unjust; but the just have cause to rejoice in their problems because God; will bring them out. There is no reason for the unjust to rejoice if there is no place in their lives for our God.

There are lots of names, but Jesus is the name to remember when you pray: God the father (Adoni, Yahweh, Jehovah), are just some of the names of God, God the son (Jesus, Yeshua) Yeshua is His Hebrew name, and the Holy Spirit! Use the name when you pray ask God to help you, He is just and will help. Here is a prayer, if you want one, it helps. Dear God, please give me the faith to believe that you can bring good out of any situation. Help me to see what you want to show me during adversity (hard times). Romans 8:28 says: "And we know that all things work together for the good for those who love God and for those who are called according to His purpose."

We have to let God use us to further the Kingdom. By helping others we help God, by serving others we show God that we Love Him. We cannot say we Love Jesus if we don't love each other and I mean with the love of God. The world doesn't know how to love like God they only know how to love themselves. This is a selfish generation of people. This young man is like the young men in the bible and there are young people like that to this day the unselfish ones, who think about Gods people first.

While it is wise to learn from the past, we shouldn't live in the past. We cannot redo or undo the past, there are no do over's in life, but by God's grace we can press forward and serve God faithfully today and in the future. The life of faith is journey forward as we become like Christ, Christ like is where the term Christians comes from!! I'm pressing forward and not backwards still praying as I'm onward bound, *"Lord, plant my feet on higher ground."* The keys to a successful walk with God; is concentration and caution, just trust Jesus and follow Him!!!

Chapter I

children; that's not good. I made the same mistake with my oldest child; I didn't talk enough about God the father and Jesus, the Son of God, and the Holy Spirit of God; the three being God all by Himself!!! The Word of God says, that we need, to teach our children day and night about the word.

This is the end of chapter 1; the next chapter is another one of my dreams and visions God gave to me. Let me just tell you a few things, before I get to the next chapter.

A lot of us call ourselves Christians and don't even know the meaning of being a Christian. First of all, being called a Christian is a privilege, not a burden. Some people walk around looking like there is something wrong all the time. Now I know that being a Christian doesn't mean that there will not be bad times in our lives, but we don't have to look like the world is coming to an end, just because something didn't turn out the way we wanted it.

God will always give us away out of anything, if we are called according to His will. Nothing will happen, unless it is in the will of God. If we are His children He will keep us from falling, if we let Him.

Bad things happen to good and bad people: Good things happen to Good and bad people. God causes it to rain on the just and the unjust; but the just have cause to rejoice in their problems because God; will bring them out. There is no reason for the unjust to rejoice if there is no place in their lives for our God.

There are lots of names, but Jesus is the name to remember when you pray: God the father (Adoni, Yahweh, Jehovah), are just some of the names of God, God the son (Jesus, Yeshua) Yeshua is His Hebrew name, and the Holy Spirit! Use the name when you pray ask God to help you, He is just and will help. Here is a prayer, if you want one, it helps. Dear God, please give me the faith to believe that you can bring good out of any situation. Help me to see what you want to show me during adversity (hard times). Romans 8:28 says: "And we know that all things work together for the good for those who love God and for those who are called according to His purpose."

We have to let God use us to further the Kingdom. By helping others we help God, by serving others we show God that we Love Him. We cannot say we Love Jesus if we don't love each other and I mean with the love of God. The world doesn't know how to love like God they only know how to love themselves. This is a selfish generation of people. This young man is like the young men in the bible and there are young people like that to this day the unselfish ones, who think about Gods people first.

While it is wise to learn from the past, we shouldn't live in the past. We cannot redo or undo the past, there are no do over's in life, but by God's grace we can press forward and serve God faithfully today and in the future. The life of faith is journey forward as we become like Christ, Christ like is where the term Christians comes from!! I'm pressing forward and not backwards still praying as I'm onward bound, *"Lord, plant my feet on higher ground."* The keys to a successful walk with God; is concentration and caution, just trust Jesus and follow Him!!!

As we trust God to rule our hearts our feet can walk His way. The church is to be a place to renew and strengthen relationships. We think that no one understands what we are going through the struggles in our lives. You need to ask God to help you find other believers with whom you can grow with. Eph. 4:11-16 says: We are meant to use our gifts to serve one another, and when we do, we accomplish the work of ministry.

Sex trafficking on American soil has become more apparent than ever. There are organizations committed to combating human trafficking estimates there are hundreds of thousands of sex trade victims in the U.S. every year. Human rebellion inflicted a mortal wound on our soul, Sin infected our total existence, marring our communion with the Lord and wreaking havoc on our social structures, marriages, and self-identity. This lethal scar pierced through every fiber of creation. If God had not acted, death would have over-whelmed us. I know you say but God didn't act or this would not be as bad as it is. But God did act, He sent Jesus to our aid, our healing arrived. Long before our Savior's incarnation, the prophet Isaiah 53:5 echoed Israel's great hope in the One to come, assuring us that "By His stripes" we would be healed. Through Jesus' cross, God applies love. Through the resurrection, Jesus heals the world. But you have to accept Jesus for who He is and trust Him. Jesus said that He came for the sick not the well. You have to know if you are sick. Everyone is sick not one is well. We are all afflicted, and the question remaining is whether or not we'll allow ourselves to be embraced by the healer.

The young man JayQuan is just the kind of person that would not just stand ideally by, and watch what was happing to the young ladies, and not do something. 1Timothy 4:12 says: Let no one treat you as if you are unimportant because you are young. Instead be an example to the believers with your words, your actions, your love, your faith, and your pure life!

The splendor of God's love gleams brightest when contrasted with the miserable mess we've made for ourselves. God is not surprised by our sad, helpless state. Jesus, with open arms wide, exhibits God's emphatic welcome to every sin-sick soul! This is why at our churches we are suppose to regularly invite people to receive prayers for healing of the body and the soul, and the spirit. Hosea 14:4 says: *"We are a people who announce good news: God will heal our waywardness and love us freely."* Following Jesus means that we are called to receive love and then give love back.

My friends encounter a love that cures. Find hope again. This is what happens when we say yes to life with God the father. We find ourselves drawn into His healing presence! Once a person is separated from the love of God, what can you do but wither and die?

The book of Proverbs is packed with practical wisdom, much of it encouraging the habit of seeking godly counsel. Proverbs 9:9-10 states: Teach the wise, and they will become even wiser; teach good people, and they will learn even more. *"Wisdom begins with respect for the Lord, and understanding begins with knowing the Holy One."* Joshua 24:15 says: *"Choose for yourselves this day who you will serve. As for me and my house we will serve the Lord!"*

God's hand of discipline is a hand of Love.

Chapter I

He's a generous God, a loving God, a kind God; He is God all by Himself! He is my all and all my (Adoni, my Elohim; my Jehovah, The One and only God. And with all the love He gives now there will be a time when He will judge us all, please make the decision to live and learn. Lord thank you for being a generous God, and remind us often; that in your generosity we are to extend that same generosity of spirit toward those around us, so that they may know who you are and rejoice in you. Praise God from whom all blessings flow!

Take JayQuan, he is an upright young man, you don't find in this world today like him, but if we would live in such a way that when people think of honesty and integrity, they will think of you. Live a good life, and encourage your friends to do so as well.

When we are engaged in God's work and we encounter setbacks, we can calmly carry on because, like the Israelites, *"We are the servants of the God of Heaven and earth."* God's Spirit gives the power to our witness.

The eyes of the Lord are on the righteous, and His ears are open to their cry. God hears us and will heal our broken hearts. Don't forget to pray for your family and friends and yourself. Jesus is the Rock, the Rock of Ages stands secure, He said He would never leave us, and He would never forsake us; and He is not a man that He should not tell the truth. Jesus will always be there when you need Him.

We honor fathers who not only gave us life, but who also show us how to live on earth. Heavenly Father, we need to know your Love in order to love others. I want to experience and share your patience and kindness with people. I want them to know that you are the reason that I can love others. Experts say that 80 percent of everything children learn in their first 12 years is through their eyes. Just think about what your children have witness over the years, will all I can say is don't be so hard on them. Teach your children the way of the Lord. Only through His strength can we reflect the Love and patience of our heavenly Father. Fathers don't frustrate your children to the point of anger; bring them up in the admonition of the Lord! Mothers, give the fathers help in bringing up the children no one can do it alone, have faith in the Lord that it will all turn out OK!!

Across the world are children who need to know of God's love for them. We can all do something, Support, Encourage, Teach, and Pray. When we love the world's children, we honor our Father in Heaven who adopted us into His family <u>Galatians 4:4-7</u>. Father, you made each child in your image, help us to convey your love to them with our hands, our help, and our hearts. The more Christ's love grows in us, the more His love flows from us.

Jesus is the Lamb of God there is no darkness in Him, so there is no darkness in those who love Him and are called by His name. He is my Lord and Savior. In the book of Revelations it talks about the lamb being the light. <u>Rev.21:23</u> The City had no need for the sun or of the moon to shine in it, for the glory of God illuminated it. The Lamb is its light. The light of the world knows no power failure. The Lord makes His face shine upon you, and be gracious to you. Thank you Lord! The Lord lifts up His countenance upon you, and gives you peace. <u>Numbers, 6:25-26</u>

A recent study shows that smiling can be good for your health. Research also shows that smiling slows down the heart and reduces stress. But smiling isn't just good for you; a genuine smile blesses those on the receiving end as well. Without a word said, it can tell other how you feel about them. Life doesn't always give us a reason to smile. But it helps those who are in pain or just feeling down. Smile today and see how many people you can make feel good! Your smile could be a message of cheer from God to a needy soul! God's training is designed to grow us in faith.

Now I'm going to tell you about another one of my visions God gave me to tell other believers about. God has giving me a lot of dreams and visions these days, some I have told in my first book and some in my second book, but some bare repeating. Now I know that you probably will not believe half of what I'm about tell you but it is TRUE, it did happen.

CHAPTER II

Like the time where God took me to heaven to see Him and I was meet by a Angel; that was at less about 12 feet tall or more. We were walking and he was taking me to see God. I saw people having picnics, and music was playing, and they were playing games and having fun, they waved at me and I waved back, and the streets were so beautiful that the shined and it was clear like glass but it was pure gold I know because I asked the Angel that was walking with me. We started passing homes, Mansions, and big houses, and little houses, and I just was in awe about it all, then we passed a door that was almost as tall as the Angel, an my name was on the door; so I stop and said oh my name is on this door can I go in, and the Angel said maybe later after we see the Master, of course, I was so inquisitive, I said well sense we are here now why not? Is it against the rule, or forbidden or something, the Angel said no; but you probably should wait because you haven't seen the Master; and He is waiting for you, so I said ok, but it will only take a minute so I pushed open the door that must have weighed a ton or two. What I saw was boxes there with my name on them, little boxes, big boxes, and they had prayers that I had prayed for, and didn't get, I started crying I said I prayed for that and I didn't get it, I prayed for that also and they were floor to ceiling and wall to wall with different things that I had prayed for, and the Angel said I told you not to see it yet , the Father wanted to give all of these things that you prayed for; but you had UNFORGIVENESS in your heart, so He said put it up, till you were ready.

You can't say you love God and still have bad feeling towards someone, or even hate someone for something that they did to you; you have to forgive because forgiveness is not for them it is for your soul. You will be free when you forgive.

Then we passed another door, oh no here I go again, and I looked in, and wall to wall floor to ceiling boxes, that had different things, dangerous things that God had saved me from. Some I knew about, and some I didn't know about, again I cried and cried. The Angel said lets go now, and see the Master. I walked a little further and saw so much light that I couldn't stand up, I felled to my knees, and cried forgive me Lord I am so sorry for not trusting you always, I love you, I do Love you so. He reach down and took my hand and helped me up and said I know you do I've seen your work on earth and I know that you love me, and then I woke up! I didn't want to wake up! I cried I wanted to go back. But the next day people looked at me and said you are just glowing what happen so I told them. You must believe that Jesus is who He says He is, and can do what He says He can do. *"Trust in the Lord at all times and lean not to your own understanding, and in all your ways acknowledge Him and He will direct your path."* My favorite scripture <u>Proverbs 3:5-6.</u>

A church, is for the believer to come, and to and get strength to make it in this sinful world, plug in for the strength of the saints, there are things that Weigh you down, in the world every day, going to work, going to the store, you are around different souls good and bad, if you are not prayed up and strong enough, the sins of the world will pull you down with it. I remember one time I was at work this was years ago and I was on my way home and one of the young ladies ask if I needed a ride to the train station; and I said think you and got in the car with her, and a couple of others that was going to the station as well, the moment I got in the car it felt different I started to feeling sick; like I couldn't breathe, so I set back in the back seat, and then she introduced the young lady that was driving as her wife. Well, I said hello, and they and the others were talking about things; and I just got sicker and sicker to my stomach. I said nothing, I knew it wouldn't take long to get there, so I couldn't breathe for a couple of miles, someone notice and I said I'm alright, I just sat there praying for God to let the traffic pick up, and to let us get there soon. Now I know you are probably thinking what was wrong, will I learn that certain demons have strong scents and strong holds over people, who have no clue, and if you are strong in the Lord, and He is your Savior and your strength; you will have powers to detect certain things in the spirit world. The smell was like a strong sulfur smell. When I got out of the car, after we got there, I jump out of the car so fast they said bye Miss Mary; I said bye thank you, but I knew that I would never ride in that car with them ever again, they had no idea what was going on in their lives. Young people please look to Jesus for your strength!

Bless the Lord Oh my soul and all that is within me; bless His Holy Name (Jesus) Psalms 103:1-5. Bless the Lord oh my soul, and forget not all His benefits. Who forgive all thy iniquities; who healed all thy diseases? Who redeems thy life from destruction, who crowns you with loving kindness and tender mercies, new mercies every morning! Thank you Lord! And who satisfies your mouth with good things, so that your youth is renewed like the eagles. In our drive to be productive for the Lord, let's remember the one thing worth being concerned about… enjoying time with our Savior! Jesus longs for our fellowship even more than we long for His.

Take JayQuan He trusted in the Lord to help him and his mother through the hurricane and God did bring them through, now I don't know if His father died or not in the hurricane, but I know that JayQuan knew Jesus as his Lord and Savior by the fruit that he showed (the way he loved people) it had to be God given strength and talent. Some of us would not have given that young lady or his friend (Carl), a second look, not even JayQuan and his mother (Juanita), could find help, if it wasn't for Jesus they would not have made it.

Softly and tenderly Jesus is calling….calling for you and for me; Patiently Jesus is waiting and watching….watching for you and for me! We plant and we water, but God gives the increase.

It was so wonderful that Robin could find a real friend who cared for her well being, and got to know the real God of love in JayQuan after knowing a snake like JayDog!! The Master restores!!!

Jesus specializes in restoration. When we become new creators in Christ, we are to put off the old man as they say the old ways, you are new now with Christ, *and be ye Christ like*! Put on the new man which is renewed in knowledge after the image of Him that created everybody! Colossians 3:8-17, the spiritual renewal from the Living God; who created us and His forgiveness, brightens the colors of our lives, while His grace sharpens the lines of His purpose for us!! The painter; and His canvas, in our lives with skilled hands, knows who and what we have been designed for in this world. No matter how bad we are, the Master artist is alive and at work within us. Thank God; for not giving up on us and for saving us, and for forgiving us, and for restoring us back to Him!!!

We are united by the very blood of Christ! We have been united together in the likeness of His death on the cross and the likeness of the resurrection. The price of our freedom from sin was paid by Jesus' blood! So if we are not willing to live our lives for Him we don't know Him as our Savior and Lord. The word says choose life or death. He has given us a choice, choose life and live with the Lord who is sitting at the right hand Of The Father. That is the less we can do for what He has done.

Wisdom from above is first pure, then peaceable, gentle, willing to yield, full of mercy James 3:17. When other people are urging us to do certain things that are questionable, we can invite God to influence our response. One is truly wise who gains his wisdom from above.

The Creator-God the Father of the universe descends into our world, sees our trouble, and offers to help. God is a very present help in time of trouble Psalms 46:1. Our Savior helps by giving us grace to endure, His Word to sustain us, friends to encourage and pray with us, and the confidence that He will ultimately work it all together for our spiritual good. *"Lord, I'm thankful that when I experience trouble in my life. You are waiting and wanting to help. Teach us to look to Jesus and to rest in His kind and loving care until He delivers us safely home again."* Amen!

When burdens weigh us down; we need to go to God's Word; one is Psalms 37:4-7. *"Delight yourself in the Lord; and He shall give you the desires of your heart."* Commit your way unto the Lord; trust in Him, and He will bring It to pass. And He shall bring forth thy righteousness as the light, and thy judgment as the noonday. Rest in the Lord, and wait patiently for Him, don't get angry with those who prosper in wicked ways. Stand means to turn our minds from its trouble thoughts of the future and to focus on God. Ask God which way to go, don't just move without knowing where you are going.

With eyes firmly fixed on Jesus Christ, resolve to walk down this road of suffering in a way that is honoring to Him. Just as He did for us at His father's request! Draw deeply on the Holy Spirit's strength for the next step you make and seek to be obedient in thought, word and deed. You will discover that as you follow Him, sweet, soul-satisfying rest will be found.

Each day as we follow Jesus Christ our Savior, we are faced with choices that will affect the lives of others. So when we choose a course of action, we should ask ourselves, does this reflect Christ's concern for others, or am I just concerned for myself? Such sensitivity, demonstrates the love of Christ that seeks to heal the broken, and help those in need. Caring for the burdens of others helps us to forget about our own.

When approaching others that don't know Jesus as their Lord and Savior is not easy but if you, *"Be wise if you will in the way you act towards them, make the most of every opportunity".* If you show kindness, love, and compassion to others, those who see us will wonder why, and that may give an opening to tell them about the beauty of the Lord's love for them. The beauty of a changed life can attract others to the One who makes us beautiful, beauty for ashes.

The church still need committed believers who teach and demonstrate a biblical mindset. To spread the gospel you need to be industrious, discipline, and persistence In order to win the world over for Jesus Christ. Focus on the Process, which is faith, virtue, knowledge, self-control, perseverance, godliness, brotherly kindness, and most of all love 2 Peter 1:5-8. Peter said if you have all of this you will be fruitful and useful in the knowledge of our Lord Jesus Christ.

God calls us to a wonderful process of learning to know Him, with the assurance that it will lead to productive service in His name and for His honor. The Christian life is a process in which we learn complete dependence on God. Stay the course and trust in the Lord!

Paul compares the Christian life as a race with a predetermined course and a finish line in eternity. Each child of God has a personalized route specially designed by the Lord. Our goal is to stay on track and run with endurance, but the path can be discerned and navigated only by focusing on Jesus. Because Jesus ran the race perfectly and finished His course, He can show us the way. As with any long-term race, the course is full of obstacles that threaten to trip or sidetrack us. Temptations lure us to what we imagine are lush green pastures, while busyness can lead us down a rabbit trail that end in exhaustion. Worry and fear grab hold of our minds, and emotions take us places the Lord never intended for us to go. Although sins present is the most obvious hindrances; other obstacles and detours a cure. Anything that takes precedence over our relationship with the Lord can send us down the wrong path. Because involvement in the daily activities of earthly life is necessary, we can easily let our families, jobs, and pleasures distract us from a wholehearted pursuit of Christ. Surprisingly, even God's blessings can become obstacles in the race if we start to pursue them more than we do the Lord Himself! We must remember that the goal is not to focus on the path or to try and find our own way. Instead, we're to fix our eyes on Jesus. He is not only our guide but also our destination. And He will welcome us home with open arms when we finish the race and cross into eternity. Hallelujah!!!! Amen!

The King is coming, If we confess our sins, He is faithful and just to forgive us our sins and to cleanse us from unrighteousness 1 John 1:9. Spiritually, when sin and failure break our relationship with God the father and sideline our service, determination alone is not what restores us to rightness with God and usefulness in His Kingdom. For us to be able to recover from our spiritual failings, we are absolutely dependent on the One who gave Himself for us. And that gives us hope. Christ, who died for us, loves us with an everlasting love and will respond with grace as we confess our faults to Him. Through confession, we can find His gracious restoration. Confession is the path that leads to restoration!!! The King is coming!!!!

You know some people still don't believe in Jesus, they think that He was just some guy who took care of people like a prophet or minister but they don't believe that He was the Son of God and still is the Son of God. Some say I don't think He was the Savior like some people think, I don't believe that He is the only way to God. Those people who rejects Him; have no clue of who they are or who God is. Just because they don't believe doesn't make it so. Many people mocked the idea that He was and is someone special. 2,000 years ago they mocked Him and put over His head the accusation written against Him: *"THIS IS THE KING OF THE JEWS"* Matthew 27:37. Those who said, *"You who destroy the temple and build it in three days, save Yourself"* verse 42. They had no idea what they were saying because He was dying for us. His death, Jesus may have seemed powerless. But when we read the whole story, we see that He gave His life willingly no one took it from Him. He proved Himself to be the Son of God and limitless in power as He burst forth from the tomb (grave). Behold the value of His death and behold the power of His resurrection. He's the Savior of the world! Jesus' resurrection put the end to death! We don't have to die, choose Jesus and Live! *"Our Casual View of Sin; Believers recognize the depravity of sin but many continue to have a careless attitude about it. We hear people say everyone sins at one time or another, so don't worry about it. Confess, and God will forgive."*

If we can be honest with ourselves about the nature of disobedience, we know the issue isn't that simple. God is faithful to forgive, but His gracious provision isn't designed as license to transgress (sin). Commandments are in place to protect us from enslavement, which is the natural result of persistent wrong-doing. Each choice to break God's rules, even as some say the *"little"* sins, adds another link in the slavery chain, we are enslaved when we sin, which eventually is long enough to wrap tightly around our heart. When that happens it hinders us from enjoying the Lord's blessing.

Any sin no matter how insignificant it seems, is rebellion against the Lord. God didn't come up with the idea of scales for wrong-doing; we did. We think a lie weighs only a little, and stealing weighs heavy; we view adultery as heavier but less substantial than murder, likewise, we reason that a lie needs only a small bit of forgiveness and grace while murder requires generous amounts of both. But God's perspective differs from our manmade notions. Jesus had to die on the cross to forgive a lie as well as murder. Though different sins cause different amounts of damage, it takes the same sacrifice to pay the penalty for theft as it does to pardon murder. We are privileged to have a Father who breaks our human chains. God offers us freedom from the domination of sin. So repent and be an obedient child of God!!! Anything other than God's plan carried out God's way and in God's timing amounts to self-reliance. Depend on His Spirit when deciding how to proceed; any other course of action can lead to serious and lasting repercussions.

Failure to listen to God; the bible tells us that *"he who neglects discipline despises himself"* while *"he who listens to reproof acquires understanding"* and *"will dwell among the wise"* <u>Proverbs 15:31-32.</u> Every time criticism comes our way, we stand at the crossroads of possibilities for good or evil. We can either embrace correction and grow up or reject it and start down the slippery slope described in <u>2Timothy 4.</u> In this passage, Paul outlines the behavior of those who become tired of hearing the truth (sound doctrine) and instead embrace the teachings of those who *"tickle"* their ears. This means they will hunt for churches or religious teachers who fail to apply the whole truth of God's word. Then they *"will turn aside to myths"*. Most people who reject some hard teachings from the bible or ignored good advice from their teachers of the word, refused to listen to God rebellion (sin). We can afford to turn away our ears even if our teachers are immature, ignorant, or evil. Because God can talk to anyone or anything, <u>Numbers 22:28</u> remember God talked to a donkey. Be mindful to keep your eyes and ears open to God's voice and word, regardless of who the word comes from. Worry is a burden that God never meant for us to bear.

As we serve each other, may we serve with the tender loving care of our Savior, encouraging each other in our spiritual journey <u>Hebrews 10:24</u>. Dear Lord, help us to be sensitive and caring as I serve others. God pours His love into our hearts to flow out to others' lives.

This Independence day, we thank God for the men and women who fought in the wars and who have been keeping the peace in the world for us. But we don't think of thanking Christ for His dying on the cross for us. Freedom is very costly; I want you to know that there is freedom in Christ! When He cried out on the cross, *"It is finished"* <u>John 19:30</u>, that's exactly what He meant. Nothing else is needed. He paid in full for yours and my salvation and promises to complete the good work He began in us <u>Phil. 1:6</u>. Adding requirements to the finished work of Christ can make people uncertain and insecure about their spiritual standing. <u>Gal 5:1</u> I have stood on for years now, *"Stand fast therefore in the liberty where Christ has made us free from sin, and do not be entangled again with the yoke of bondage."* Keep your freedom do not go back into the slavery of sin.

Jesus says: *"If you Love me you will keep my commandments."* <u>John 15:5</u> *"I am the vine, you are the branches. He who abides in Me, and I in Him, bears much fruit; for without Me you can do nothing."*

John 15:13 *"Greater love has no man than this that he lay down his life for his friends."* We are totally and eternally dependent on the One who died to set us free. For Christian Independence Day is actually Dependence Day! Our greatest strength comes from dependence on our strong God. Grow in the grace and knowledge of our Lord and Savior Jesus Christ! St Peter viewed spiritual growth as a defense against teaching that incorrectly interprets God's Word and leads people astray.

Even when we feel discourage and disconnected from God, we can remember that, He will help us advance in our faith, by making us more like His Son. His Word assures us that *"He who has begun a good work in us will complete it until the day of Jesus Christ"* Phil1:6. Dear God, I invite Your Holy Spirit to mold me and shape me into the person You want me to be. Spiritual growth requires the solid food of God's Word!

The Lord said, *"Stand in the ways and see, and ask for the old paths, where the good way is, walk in it; then you will find rest for your souls. But they said, 'We will not walk in it"* Jeremiah 6:16. Jeremiah made known that this was the word from God not his words, but the people would not listen. They wanted to walk their own way, and then they wonder why God punished them. Judah had turned away from the Lord, just as people today have. God can teach us from our past that the best road is the one we walk with Him. God's guidance in the past gives courage for the future. Stay on the right path with Jesus!

And please stay away from unbelievers who are always ready to give believers advice. Too often we find the world's methods and wisdom attractive. Divine direction is needed if we are to set ourselves apart from nonbelievers thinking and yet stay close enough to be able to share God's viewpoint and His message of hope to the world. God declares that His grace is sufficient to keep us going in every situation. That means we need never give up. The Grace to keep Going; those who've been rescued from sin are best able to help rescue others. These are uncertain times that we are in. So *"Let the peace of God, which surpasses all understanding, guard your hearts and minds through Christ Jesus"* Phil.4:7. Believers in Jesus can have peace in the midst of uncertainties; because we have the assurance that our heavenly Father loves His children and cares for our needs Matt.6:25-34. Our peace comes from the confidence that the Lord loves us and He is in control. He alone provides the comfort that settles our nerves, fills our minds with hope, and allows us to relax even in the midst of changes and challenges. *You will keep him in perfect peace whose mind is stayed on You* Isaiah 26:3. Trust Him He knows best!!!

The Lord God says *"My grace is sufficient for you; for my strength is made perfect in your weakness"* 2Corin.12:9. So don't let the devil fool you, you can make it, with the strength of Jesus. We have the *Holy Spirit* the *Power* we need to endure. Trusting in God's grace helps us believe that God will bring good from our troubles Rom.8:28. Then with the trust our focus shifts from our trials to the Lord. We trust that God will bring us through, with deeper intimacy and greater faith in the end. *God is Sovereign!* The Apostle Paul had been through shipwrecks, imprisonment, and beatings-difficulties far worse than what most of us face. Yet he didn't quit, because he drew on God's grace and mercy and found it sufficient for every circumstance.

I'm teaching the cross, the meaning of the cross. Jesus in His perfect life was the only one who could redeem us from our sins. Our Savior left heaven to dwell on earth and become one of us. He obediently accomplished the work of His Father John 5:19. He alone was qualified to be our substitute and bear God's judgment for our sins. As we know three days later He arouse from the dead. My Savior's sacrifice on the cross was accepted as payment in full for our sins. And now He has open the door to all who trust in Jesus, Our resurrected Lord, having appeared on the earth to many people, ascended to live forever with His Father, and made a way for us to dwell in heaven with Him someday. At its heart is Calvary, the place where Jesus died so we could be forgiven. We see that the cross symbolizes Salvation Sacrifice, and Service. Jesus accomplished all for us and nothing else is needed. He gave His life as a ransom; for all Mark 10:45. *"Jesus said that He came to serve not to be served."* Our Savior calls us to be obedient and to deny ourselves and follow Him through sacrificial service to others Luke 9:23. As we embrace a life-style of humility and servant hood, we will bring glory to our Heavenly Father!!! But Greatness in God's Kingdom is found in the life of obedience. I hope you are following His plan and helping others as Jesus did.

God is Sovereign. God is All-Powerful. God is Love. And God knows what He is doing. Our greatest comfort in sorrow is to know that *God is in Control!!!!*

I will lift up my eyes to the hills, from which comes my help! My help comes from the Lord, who made heaven and earth. Amen! He preserves us from evil and keeps us safely in His care for all eternity. In faith we lift our eyes up to the One who is our Redeemer and Creator. He is our help and our hope for now and forever more till eternity. Christ was lifted up that He might lift us up. Humble yourselves in the sight of the Lord, and He shall lift you up. Amen!!! James 4:10. Who is your Master?

No man or woman is absolutely free. Roman 6:16 says we are slaves of who ever we obey-slaves either to sin (the devil) or disobedience (self) or to the three people you love more (me, myself, and I), or obedience to the Lord. Every human is born with a fallen nature, being the master of our own life is the same as being enslaved to sin; that's scary, because Our Heavenly Father's prescription for this unhealthy situation is submission to Him. But we often think to ourselves, if I give the Lord control, then I lose it (Hallelujah) and that's scary to me. God could lead me (somewhere I need to be but don't want to go). When fear seeps into your heart, stop and think the Lord's character and motives: Holy and sinless! He has infinite wisdom, perfect knowledge. What's more He loves you and has the power to work all things together for your good. Now compare your credentials to His. Who do you think would make a better Master of your life!!!! Will I hope you can answer that honestly!

The Holy Spirit will not fill believers who tolerate sin in their lives. The grace of God covers the guilt of our transgressions, but it cannot and will not be used to excuse continued disobedience Romans 6:1-2. We grieve the Spirit when we say yes to sin, and stifle Him when we say no to God, Eph.4:30; 1Thess. 5:19. None of us can attain sinless perfection on earth, but each time we take a step towards obedience, our walk gets lighter and lighter, sin can't control us when we are obedient to God, allow Him to order your steps. Press on you'll soon begin to live in the freedom of enslavement to the most wonderful and amazing Master you have ever known.

Colossians 3:16-17 says *let the words of Christ dwell in you richly in all wisdom; teaching and admonishing one another in psalms and hymns and spiritual songs, singing with grace in your hearts to the Lord. And whatsoever you do in word or deed, do all in the name of the Lord Jesus, giving thanks to God and the Father by Him!! Amen!*

I'd like to take a little time to talk about forgiveness. I know we all say what's to forgive. It's too painful or it's not me it's him or her. God forgave us so we are to forgive them it's simple isn't it? To forgive means *"to give up all claims to punish or exact a penalty for an offense".* No strings or conditions can be attached, or else it ceases to be a pardon (forgiven). Neither salvation nor forgiveness can be earned, both must be freely given. God granted us forgiveness and we did not deserve and could not earn. Unforgiveness is emotional bondage that consumes minds with memories of offenses, distorts emotions with revenge, and fills hearts with churning unrest. Its tentacles reach deep into the soul, affecting the spirit and the body health wise. But the one who chooses to put on love and offer forgiveness is ready to receive the peace of Christ. Let God's Word help you release hurt and anger into His caring and holy hands, then watch as vengeful thoughts are transformed into praise and gratitude to the Lord. This present of forgiveness cannot be manufactured in ourselves, we need God, and He wrapped this gift in the love of God with the red ribbon of Christ's sacrifice. It is freely given to us by the Savior, and our job is to simply pass it on to others. There are some people who you might say are fools (among other things, a person who lacks sense or judgment) and we have to deal with them but the bible says in Proverb 18 especially than a fool has no delight in understanding you cannot reason with a fool. And also the words of a man or woman's mouth are as deep as waters, but wisdom is like a flowing stream, words do hurt it goes deep. The words of fools start quarrels. They make you want to beat them. And a fool only delights in what they say not what you say, they only want to tell others what they think.

Daniel 9:9 says *"To the Lord our God belong mercies and forgiveness, new mercies every day, thank God for new mercies."*

The name of the Lord is a strong tower; the righteous can run to Him for safety Prov. 18:10. *God is: Elohim, the God above all gods; Jehovah Jireh, the God who provides; El-Shaddai, the Almighty God; Jehovah Rapha, God our healer; Jehovah Shalom, our God of peace; Jehovah Shamma, our God who is present; Jehovah Yahweh, our loving, covenant-keeping God and there are many more names and characters. But He is God all by Himself!* Lord, remind us that; *Your* name reveal, *Your* character. Help us to remember them in our times of need and distress. Thank You for the assurance that, You are faithful to Your name. God's names, which describe His character, can bring comfort when we need it most.

A good thing to think about is what if there was no grace! Think about each of us would be called to account immediately for every indiscretion. There would be no time for repentance or change of behavior. There would be no forgiveness. No mercy. No hope. Living in this world sometimes feels like we are falling into a no-grace sinkhole. When people refuse to overlook the faults and offenses of others, we end up burdened by the weight of guilt that we were never meant to carry. God, in His grace, sent Jesus to carry the burden for us (when we repent). Those who receive God's gift of grace have the privilege of offering it to others on Christ's behalf: *"Above all things have fervent love for one another, for 'love will cover a multitude of sins'"* 1Peter4:8. When we gracefully acknowledge the grace we've received, we joyfully give it to those in need!

Why is it so challenging for us to follow a godly path? Well there are two conflicting tendencies that exist in every believer: the patterns of the corrupted old self, "the flesh" and the righteousness of a new nature in Christ. The quality of forgiveness, or lack of it, will largely determine which tendency prevails in our lives. The inevitable result of unforgiveness is anger, bitterness, and malice. By refusing to forgive, we allow the old flesh nature to dominate and produce its poisonous fruit. Every area of our life is affected when we refuse to extend to others the pardon Christ so generously extended to us; in essence, we are treating those around us as we would never want the Lord to treat us. Thankfully, His mercy toward us has no limit. Forgiveness frees us to live in our new Christ like nature and enables us to see others through eyes of grace and mercy. Something has to change let it be you!

God forgives everyone who trusts Christ as Savior. With His blood, Jesus paid our entire sin debt and obtained our full pardon Matt. 26:28. Every sin without exception is covered Col. 2:13-14. Forgiveness is given to everyone who believes in Jesus Acts 10:43 and remains available to all believers 1 John 1:9. Our pardon for sin is based on the riches of our Father's grace, which always exceeds the offense Eph. 1:7; Rom. 5:20. To reconcile us to Himself, God sent His Son to die in our place. He accepted Christ's sacrifice as payment in full for our transgressions. He offers forgiveness solely on the basis of our relationship with His Son Jesus, not on our behavior. This isn't license to sin…far from it! Divine forgiveness should instead motivate a passion for holiness!!!! Amen!

This is one of the ironies of faith: God uses the insignificant to accomplish the great. Not many of us are wise or noble; most of us are anonymous and far from extraordinary. Yet all of us can be used by God. And contrary to what we might think, it is because of our weakness that we can be used by God <u>1Cor.1:27-29; 2Cor. 12:10.</u> When we are weak He is strong. By God's great power, we can do all that He has called us to do. To experience God's power, we must first admit that we are weak.

The believer who spends time with the Father can expect rich rewards. King David's psalms often speak of the stillness of soul and renewed energy that he experienced from time in God's presence. Our spirit is quieted in prayer so that worry and frustration are soothed away. As the Lord refreshes us inwardly, we can feel the tension melt from our muscles. Not even a poet like David can explain how it happens, but the result of our worship is divine energy surging through these human bodies. Our emotions are renewed as well. In spite of the great rewards that result from spending time in God's presence, many Christians avoid it—especially when they are trying to ignore sin in their life. But He is determined to purify our hearts so we can be conformed to the image of His Son. If we are afraid of His correction, and resist the transformation process, our relationship with Him will weaken. On the other hand, a desire to deal with anything that interferes with our connection to the Father will lead to a closer personal walk and bring blessings that go with being His beloved child. Time spent in His presence is always rewarded.

True Loyalty!" If I must boast, I will boast in the things which concern my infirmity" <u>2Corin.11:30.</u> Whether we receive persecution or praise for our service to the Lord, may our focus always be loyalty to Him and gratitude for His sacrifice of Love. I am Yours, Lord, yet teach me all it means, all it involves of love and loyalty, of Holy service, full and glad, in unreserved obedience to You!! Our loyalty to Jesus grows from His love for us.

Praying past our attitude! There are three crucial areas that we may need to work on before we approach the throne of God. **First**, we must come to our Father submissively: bowing before Him in humility and thanking Him for His accessibility. **Second**, we must trust God: knowing that He will guide us in the right direction and never steer us down a wrong path. **Third**, we must be thankful in our speech and mindset: Showing Him we recognize and appreciate the countless blessings He has bestowed upon us. We can demonstrate as with an *"attitude of gratitude."* When we come to the throne of God in submission, trust, and gratitude, we are going to hear the truth from our caring Father. But if these characteristics are not present in our life, we may miss His message. Prayerfully consider your attitude with regard to these three areas, asking the Lord to realign you heart and mind with His perfect will! Amen!

Do you feel chained to difficult circumstances? God can give you contentment. Lasting satisfaction can be found only with Him, for in His *"presence is fullness of joy; at His right* hand *are pleasures forevermore"* Ps 16:11. When all you have is God you have all you need.

Most of us like to look good. We want to appear that we have it all together with no struggles or fears or temptation or heartaches. Trying to maintain a façade of perfection on our spiritual journey doesn't help us or our fellow travelers. But sharing our lives, with others in the body of Christ benefits us as well as others; and as we enjoy a growing fellowship with God and become more aware of our own brokenness and inadequacy, God is able to use us more fully to help others. *"Let us consider one another in order to stir up love and good works"* Heb.10:24. Believers stand strong when they don't stand alone.

Sometimes past disappointments at times cause us to feel little hope for the future, and financial pressures, declining health, and painful relationships can also take an emotional toll on us. When we are discouraged, our first priority should be to cry out to our heavenly Father. Let's take our disappointments to the Lord in prayer, why not He is going to be up all night anyway! He is the only one who can help us in any situation, trust Him call Him, He will answer. He is and always will be a prayer answering God! We can't let discouragement come over us and affect us like there is no tomorrow, because first our mind becomes divided. We have difficulty concentrating, no matter where we are or who is with us, we keep thinking about the disappointment. Then we start blaming others for our disappointment and it may be so but there may be that it is our own fault but we like to place blame on others for our disappointments in life. We may even start blaming God for our trials. Then we start focusing on what we dislike or don't have, and anger can occur; we lash out because people or circumstances have failed us. Then we start driving people away and discouragement leads to unwise decisions, and a divided mind, and a wrong focus, a negative attitude and in unresolved anger. We won't think clearly or act in God-pleasing manner. So before things get out of hand please stop and pray to God for guidance. After praying, we must look to God in anticipation of what He will do. The Lord moved the heart of many people, who showed favor toward us. God will move and send people

Chapter II

to help us in discouraging times. Will you look to the Lord in hope and accept the assistance He sends? Please trust God in every way, He knows what we need.

Blessed is the man, woman, and or child that trust in the Lord! Jeremiah 17:7. Like a firmly rooted tree, people who trust in God have a sense of stability and vitality despite the worst circumstances. In contrast, people who place their trust in the wrong places like other people often live with a sense of instability. *The Bible compares these people to a desert shrub that are frequently malnourished and stand alone* Jer.17:6. Where are our roots? Are we rooted in Jesus? Are we a bridge that leads others to Him? If we know Christ, we can testify to His truth! Even strong trials cannot blow down a person who is rooted in God.

"Jesus Christ is the same yesterday, today and forever." This can lift our hearts above our daily trials to remind us that an unchanging, trustworthy God rules over even the chaos of a changing world. Let the sameness of God waft over your heart with His peace in your storms.

God doesn't call us to find fulfillment in the amount of work we do for Him or the number of people who are a part of that work, but in faithfully doing our work for His sake. Serving our great God with His strength in a small way is not a stepping-stone to greatness—it is greatness. Anyone doing God's work in God's way is important in His sight!

To delight yourself in the Lord: means to take pleasure in discovering more about God and following His will. Spending time with the Father—learning what pleases Him and praying for discernment to make wise decisions-has two results. **First** the Holy Spirit aligns our heart's desires with Scripture; and **second**, we set ourselves up for blessing. Delight in God derives from dedication to Him. When we commit our way to the Lord, we allow His will and mandates to shape our thoughts, lifestyle, and goals. God's word will not fail us, it says in Psalms 27:9, 11"*For evildoers shall be cut off; but those that wait on the Lord, they shall inherit the earth. But the meek shall inherit the earth; and shall delight themselves in the abundance of peace.* Amen! God promises to give us our heart's desires in His time when our requests are aligned with His will. Claim the promises as written, and He will bless you richly.

Believers can have wrong desires. In fact, if we work hard enough-by pressing ahead of divine timing (such as Sarai and Abram, before they became Sarah and Abraham Genesis 16:1-5), manipulating our circumstances, and even acting dishonestly—we may be able to make those wishes reality. But anything gained apart from God will prove to be empty and disappointing. Having desires is good—-goals drive us and set the direction for our life. But we want our objectives to match the ones God has for us. Desires contrary to His purposes have the power to corrupt the body, mind and spirit and can also cause believers to fall into temptation 2Peter 2:9-10; 1 Timothy 6:9.

How can we be sure our desires are right? A godly ambition is usually specific and fixed, and it will stand up to evaluation through prayer and bible study. On the other hand, a wrong desire fails to meet these criteria. For instance, some people have only a vague sense of what they want from life. Or they change their minds about what they want as time passes. Most dangerous is that goal which is pursued despite its incompatibility with a righteous lifestyle. In those cases the believer as fail to consider two vital questions: Does God want this for me?

And can I follow Christ and this objective at the same time? Many of the things we desire are not specifically addressed in Scripture as *"thou shalt"* or *"thou shalt not."* That is why God has given us access to the Holy Spirit's wisdom and discernment. We must prayerfully evaluate our longings to ensure we are within the Lord's will and pursuing His purpose for our life.

He who believes in Me, as the Scripture has said, out of his heart will flow rivers of living water John 7:38. Christ is, after all, the living water for whom people are thirsting. Jesus is a never-ending supply of living water for a parched world. There is enough water for the whole world.

The Lord chooses unexceptional people like Peter and you and me to build His kingdom. He asks His followers to love Him above all else and fully commit to obeying Him. When we do, He will accomplish more through us than we could ever imagine.

It is only from God that we can receive the grace of forgiveness when our choices have produced painful regrets. And only in Him do we find the wisdom to make better choices. *Father of mercies; forgive me for the foolish choices I have made. Please enable me to be wiser in my choices. Teach me the value of resting in Your grace.* God's forgiveness frees us from the chains of regret.

The Precious Blood of Jesus Christ! John 1:13 says: *They meaning (us) did not become His children in any human way by any human parents or human desire. They were born of God.* This is a definite statement that no one becomes a child of God because of his parents, or through any blood stream. Salvation or Christianity is not passed down to the children through the blood stream of the father or mother. Each child and each relative must experience the will and the Power of God in his own personal case in order to become a child of God. This relationship only comes about through personal faith in Jesus Christ!

1John 1:7 says: *But if we walk in the light, as He is in the light, we have fellowship one with another and the blood of Jesus Christ His Son cleaned us from all sin.* The Blood here represents the sacrifice of Christ at Calvary with all the saving Power connected with it. When we Believe in and trust the Lord Jesus Christ; God and Christ apply His sacrifice to our record of sins, and to ourselves in order to blot out all these sins and iniquities. God has made a *"blood bank."* Any person who believes in and accepts the Lord Jesus Christ may and does receive the benefits of that Precious Blood!

According to Paul he instructed Timothy to establish priorities in the church, and prayer was first on the list. Paul said pray for Kings and all who are in authority 1Tim.2:2. The reason for this is so we can live peaceable lives and godly lives and thereby have unhindered opportunity to share the Savior with others. Our problem is not with the Lord's promise or capability, but with our lack of faith. By focusing on the problems or the power of those in office, we lose sight of our Sovereign God who waits for us to request His intervention. Pray for the nation and the people in office. Political policies and legislation are not ultimately determined in conference rooms and governmental chambers, but in prayer closets. The voices that shape this nation are not necessarily those in legislative halls, but those that approach the throne room of God with bold faith. As the church believes and prays, the Lord will respond. Everyone says if God could change things then why has He waited so long, and He may be asking you the same question: "Why have you waited so long to pray?" Every authority on earth can be touched by the power of prayer if we are willing to ask and believe God.

God promises to give us long life if we are obedient to His word and His commandments. From God's point of view it is far more than just trying to be good. It is always about relationship—relationship in which surrender is the way we express our grateful love to Him. Jesus, in amazing love for us, surrendered Himself on the cross to recue us from our helpless bondage to sin and set us on a journey to all that is good and glorious. Surrender is God's love language. This is how we show Him our love for Him!!! Amen!

He counts the number of the stars; He calls them all by name. *"The Lord lifts up the humble" and takes pleasure in those who fear Him, in those who hope in His mercy." He loves us so much that "He gave His only begotten Son, that whoever believes in Him should not perish but have everlasting life"* John3:16. God, who knows the name of every star, knows all our names as well. Amen!

We were created to be members of God's family and recipients of His perfect love. In fact, through the sacrifice of His Son Jesus, He demonstrated just how much He loves us. Consider the Roman centurion who asked Jesus to heal his servant. Seeing the man's genuine faith, the Lord granted his request out of love for him Luke 7:2-10. Jesus extended forgiveness to the thief on the cross, who placed his faith in Christ Luke 23:39-43. Before his conversion, Saul of Tarsus was convinced that Jesus was not the promised Messiah and His followers must be stopped. God's love did not even skip over one so violently opposed

Dreams and Visions

to His children. On the road to Damascus, the Lord appeared to Saul with an offer of salvation and gave him a great work to do—evangelizing the Gentile world <u>Acts 9:15.</u> The human mind cannot fully comprehend divine love. In Christ, thieves, persecutors, and those who may look like outsiders are all equally loved.

God guide our steps toward and not away from those who need You. Then guide our words and our actions so that we can be purposeful in our encounters with others. God's good news is too good to keep to ourselves. A God of Love; the Lord does not base His love for us upon our character or achievements, thank God. The Savior's dealings with people show us the depth of God's love. Judas Iscariot, one of Jesus' 12 disciples, ministered closely with the Lord for three years but in the end chose to betray Him. Even though Jesus knew what Judas would do, Jesus never rejected him. In Love, the one betrayed forgave the betrayer. Next, consider Peter, who loved Jesus and desired to follow Him always. In a moment of weakness, however, he denied even knowing Christ. Though Jesus knew in advance the disciple would do this, His love for the man didn't waver one bit, a fact He proved by appearing to Peter after the resurrection and giving him a prominent place in the developing church. A crocked tax collector and a Samaritan woman caught in adultery didn't stop Jesus from loving them. He forgave them and offered His loving forgiveness. Through faith in Jesus, everyone even the worst of sinners can become a child of God and experience the richness of His love. No one is beyond its reach.

<u>Isaiah 17:1, 7-11.</u> He says, *"Because you have forgotten the God of your salvation, (talking to the people in the cities) the harvest will be a heap of ruins."* This prophecy serves as a warning about the danger and

futility of thinking we can produce anything on our own. Apart from God, the work of our hands will become a pile of ruins. But when we join with God in the work of *His* hands, God multiplies our effort and provides spiritual nourishment for many. Lord, we want to be a part of what You are doing in Your world. Apart from you, our work is nothing. Lead us fill us, use us. Nourish others through us. *"Without God you can do nothing!"*

What we believe determines how we will act. To behave in a godly manner, we must embrace biblical truth. Man's relationship was broken; apart from Jesus Christ death on the cross solved that. *Salvation comes through Jesus alone* Acts 4:12. *The church…Christ's body….is made up of born-again believers throughout the world* 1 Corin.12:13. All Christians are commanded to worship the Lord, care for one another, and share in the work of spreading the gospel. God's followers are also given spiritual gifts to use in building up other believers. Forgiving others will become a possibility and dying to self a more common occurrence. *Ungodly traits will fade away and be replaced by the fruit of the Spirit* Gal. 5:22-23.

Those who don't show any regard for God may seem to prosper at the moment, but God will ultimately right all wrong. God acts Sovereignty in all that comes to pass so that everything works toward His good purpose. God's plan will surely take place and be on schedule. We can't sort out the whole picture from where we are in life; only God can. So let us continue to live by faith and not by sight. From His perspective, all things are working together for the believer's good and for His honor. Sovereign Ruler of the skies; ever gracious, ever wise; our times are in God's hands; our souls are in His keeping.

Being busy working for the Lord is good, but Jesus said there is something better…..As Martha worked diligently to prepare a meal for Jesus and His disciples, her sister Mary sat at Jesus feet and listened. Martha's work was needed, but it was not the most important thing. Jesus said, "Mary has chosen *what is better, and it will not be taken away from her"*Luke 10:42.

Every follower of Jesus can be consistent giver and receiver of courage. The Lord can use us today to encourage and strengthen each other. When people share their fears with you, share your courage with them, *"God's Scriptural Benefit package."*

God's plans for you do not stop at salvation. His goal is that you become conformed to the likeness of His Son, and the tool He uses is the Bible. The foundation is laid with the teaching of Scripture's basic truths. These doctrines about God's character and work anchor our souls during the storms of life and protect us from deception. Since we all have certain flesh patterns, perfection is impossible, and we sometimes fall into sin. But when Scripture offers reproof, we are convicted about our wrongdoing. Now this is followed by correction. The Lord never convicts us and leaves us in the mess we have made. He provides what we need to make things right. The final step is training in righteousness. Think of this as a one-on-one discipleship course with the Word of God. If we heed the instruction and discipline of Scripture, we'll grow in obedience and godliness and eventually will find that we need less reproof and less correction. Full participation in God's Scriptural benefit package involves three things: Read the bible each day. Believe everything God says in His Word…not just the parts you like

Heb 4:2 and do what He says. You will become equipped and qualified to fulfill His purpose for you, in life.

We have access to the throne, we must come with boldness to the throne ask what you want and need He will give it to you if you have been walking in His commandments, if you have been obedient to His will. Confident Access is what we have, don't waste it Heb. 4:16. Because of Jesus' death and resurrection, we can now approach God with fear. God's penalty for sin has been satisfied, and we are invited into God's presence. Because of Jesus we can come to God through prayer anywhere, anytime. Then boldly let our faith address God's throne of grace and mercy. Through prayer, we have instant access to our Father!

Have you been crying out to the Father for more of Him? Do you need to know God's will for a particular area of your life? Biblical fasting is a spiritual discipline that will bring you to the place where your hearing is sharper, your mind is clearer, and your eyes are more firmly fixed on the Lord and His plans. Many of us have not tried fasting because it seems too foreign to us. We don't know how to begin or when to find the time. But if we see it for what it is, a faith experience that sharpens our spiritual vision intensifies our desire for God and leads us to better understanding His direction, and then we will want to try it for ourselves. When you fast don't tell everyone, and don't go around looking like you are dying wash your face and anoint yourself, so you will be able to concentrate on the task at hand (fasting). You will get closer to God and feel His presence. You will know His will for your life; which is just what you want right, a closer walk with the Master. Many people testify that God has used biblical fasting to position their hearts to receive

His truth. It has made them ready for the planting of the Word, and through that, to receive greater insight and direction, and to develop a deeper faith Romans 10:17. During the hours of fasting, they set themselves apart from earthly concerns and spent their time concentrating on heavenly matters. It was then that God revealed the stumps, rocks, and thick roots that entangled their hearts and prevented spiritual growth. Through His Spirit, He also provided the courage to confess and the strength to obey. God desires to clear out the rocks and weeds on our lives and break up any hard soil; biblical fasting prepares us for such tilling. God is calling His people to consecrate themselves to Him.

In 1 John 3:1, John affirms that we are indeed part of God's family by saying, *"Behold what manner of love the Father has bestowed on us, that we should be called children of God!"* He then describes the trademarks of those who are the children of God, including, *"Beloved, let us love one another, for love is of God; and everyone who loves is born of God and knows God"* 1 John 4:7. Because we are children of God "Love is of God;" the chief way to reflect the heart of the Father is by displaying the love that characterizes Him. May we allow His Love to reach out to others through us! Father, teach us to love with the love of Christ that others might see Your love reflected in my care and concern for them. Love is the family resemblance the world should see in followers of Christ!

Believers are called to be sanctified people who live holy lives. Holiness means being set apart by God for His purposes. This process of sanctification begins when we receive Jesus Christ as our personal Savior, and it continues for the rest of our lives. The Holy Spirit draws our will and longings to align with His. As we submit to Him, we will begin to desire what He desires. With His leading, we will choose to consecrate our conduct, our conversation, and ultimately our character to God alone. He teaches us how to make holiness a way of life rather than see it as some lofty place of enlightenment we can never reach. God has placed us where we live and work, not to be "pious" or to isolate ourselves as if in incubators, but to reflect who Christ is as we walk among other people. If we are in the process of being conformed to Jesus' likeness, then the longer we live and mature spiritually, the more others should be able to recognize the Savior in us. Our hearts should grow softer, and our willingness to love and serve should increase.

If we are Christ's ambassadors, then our lives must be holy; otherwise, we are misrepresenting Him. If we are the body of Christ, then our hands are His hands, our eyes His eyes, and our feet His feet. When we allow Jesus to speak, love, and serve through us, others will be compelled to ask why we live such vibrant lives. All followers of Christ are called to be holy. To answer this call daily is to embrace the Great Commission.

Incline your ear, and come to Me. Hear, and your soul shall live Isaiah 55:3. In His Word, the Lord encourages us to seek Him: *"Seek the Lord while He may be found, call upon Him while He is near"* Isaiah 55:6. He calls to our hearts. Because of Jesus' death and resurrection, we can come to Him right now and will one day go into eternity to be with Him forever. Just as I am......I come! *"Let Him who thirsts come. Whoever desires let him take the water of life freely"* Revelation 22:17.

Now this is the end of chapter II

CHAPTER III

So now let me tell you about another dream God gave me. One day I was on the bus with a friend, going somewhere I don't remember where exactly, but I remember that we must be on the wrong bus, because the streets and building didn't look familiar. So we got off; and then there were some young men in the front of this store. Now all of a sudden, lots of young men trying to scare people and bully them, so some of the boys surrounded me, and said give me your bag lady. I wasn't about to give them my purse, so I said go home, you need to stop trying to scare people, does your parents know that you are out here trying to scare and bully everyone? Why are you doing this? They said look old lady we need money for food: I said well all you had to do is ask, they said we don't ask for nothing we take what we want.

So I said hear is all the money I have and I am not giving you my purse, so take it and leave, so they did, and I heard them say you're a dumb old lady, and I said thank you go home now, let these people alone. They left and I went in the store around the back because it was so hectic in the front and so many people that I couldn't get in. So I see a man in the back taking out the trash and I ask him could I come in to make a call for someone to pick me up, and he said sure lady come. So now I go in; and it's a little dark back here, there were tables, and I guess candle on the tables, like a restaurant. I'm thinking this man has it made at a time when people are hungry; he has a restaurant in the back and a market in the front.

The people were shouting things like I was here first in line get back, I will take that piece, one leg, and one breast over there and I'll take that thigh. I'm getting closer to the front after I made my call. So now I see brown paper very thin paper that they are using to wrap up the meat, but I have never seen such thin kind of paper before, and so I say thank you and start walking to the front door there were people all outside the door and all down the street. I said WOW! I'm thinking and then I turn as I was going out the door and I saw that the paper was the skin of humans and I look at the counter and it was a big glass case of parts that were human a human leg and thigh and a human arm and breasts and I didn't see a head but I just kept walking very fast like I didn't see anything and the people act as if they didn't see me either, then I woke up and I said Lord why did you give me this dream and He said so you could tell everyone about the last days on earth. The end times as they talk about in the bible. It's also known as the Lord's Day!

For nation shall rise against nation, and kingdom against kingdom: and there shall be famines, and pestilences, and earthquakes, in divers' places Matthew 24:7. Jesus is talking and He said when we see this that is the beginning of the end. I for one will not be here to see such a thing. But if I am here Jesus promises that His people will be protected, so we have nothing to fear, because God in His infinite mercy will keep His children safe as He did in the wilderness after the Exit from Egypt!

We read in Psalms 59:16-17, *"I will sing of your power; yes, I will sing aloud of Your mercy in the morning; for You have been my defense and refuge in the day of my trouble. To You, O my Strength, I will sing praises; for God is my defense, my God of mercy."* For the hurting heart of every generation, our *"city of refuge"* is not a place. Our city of refuge is a Person, the God who loves us with an everlasting love. May we find our refuge and rest in Him! Refuge can be found in the Rock of Ages.

"Fully Alive," 1 Corin.15:22 read; *for as in Adam all die, even so in Christ shall all be made alive!* Paul pointed out that before the Lord rescued us, we were spiritually dead. But once we received Jesus as our Savior, we became *alive in Him* Romans 6:11. Paul wanted us to realize that we have a new freedom, a new nature, and a new standard of conduct.

Together they provide a starting point for us to grasp the glorious foundational truth of being alive in the Lord! Only through the teaching of the Holy Spirit can we begin to comprehend its full meaning. Besides God's living Word is meant to be experienced. We can know the fact that Jesus has given us a new nature, but only when we experience this new nature and the freedom it brings do we truly discover the scriptural meaning of *"made alive."* Spiritual joy will fill your being as you experience the truth of the revealed mystery of being fully alive in Christ! *Marvel not at this; for the hour is coming, in which all that are in their graves shall hear His voice, and shall come forth; they that have done good, (will rise and have life forever) unto the resurrection of life; and they that have done evil, (will rise and be judged guilty) unto the resurrection of damnation* John 5:28-29.

But God's free gift is not like Adam's sin. Many people died because of the sin of the one man. But the grace from God was much greater; many people received God's gift of life by the grace of the one man, Jesus Christ. After Adam sinned once, he was judged guilty. But the gift of God is different. God's free gift came after many sins and it makes people right with God. One man sinned, and sin's death ruled all people because of that one man. But now those people who accept God's full grace and great gift of being made right with Him will surely have true life and rule through the one man, Jesus Christ. So as one sin of Adam brought the punishment of death to all people, one good act that Christ did makes all people right with God. And that brings true life for all. One man disobeyed God, and many became sinners. In the same way, one man obeyed God, and many will be made right. The law came to make sin worse. But when sin grew worse, God's grace increased. Sin once used death to rule us, but God gave people more of His grace so that grace could rule by making people right with Him. And this brings life forever through Jesus Christ our Lord Romans 5:15-21!

Think of the blessing of being in God's Graceland. It is a realm where He has given us entrance into His presence and where that same grace continues to overflow into our lives on a daily basis. Paul tells us that even in times of despair God showers us with sufficient grace to see us through 2 Corin. 12:9. No matter what life may bring, nothing can remove us from the realm of God's grace. Lord, for the blessings of Your grace I am forever grateful! Teach me to accept Your grace and to live in its power. Help me to share Your story with others. Remember where you live and rejoice in His grace.

Knowing that we would need a way to understand Him, our heavenly Father revealed Himself through His Son. And so *"the Word became flesh, and dwelt among us"* John 1:14. The better we get to know Jesus, the more we will understand the Father John 14:9. And when we take a look at the way Jesus treated people around Him, we get a good illustration of God's Love. The Lord does not want us burdened by guilt, shame, or heartache. Nor does He want us to be secluded from other people. Instead, He calls us to become active participants in His kingdom. Have you cut yourself off from those around you? Take hold of your Savior's hand today, and start experiencing the joy of His acceptance.

We are all one in Christ Jesus Galatians 3:28, a shared bond. In some places, meeting another believer is not unusual because there are many believers. It's thrilling to share together the amazing reality of the freedom from sin we have through Christ! For all who know Jesus, there is a shared bond, aloneness in Christ, a joy of fellowship that can brighten even the darkest day. Praise God that He brings a bond of unity to all who know Him as Savior. *What a miracle it is, dear Lord, that You can bring together people of all tribes, tongues, and nations to be like-minded in Christ…to share a bond of love and affection for Jesus!* Christian fellowship builds us up and binds us together.

We can feel good about ourselves, but that confidence must come from the knowledge that we're greatly loved children of God John 3:16, not that we're very good children Rom 7:18. The first step in becoming a truly "good" person as a follower of Christ is to stop pretending that we're good on our own and to ask God to make us as good as we can be. We will fail many times, but He will keep growing us and changing us. God is faithful and in His time and in His way, He'll do it.

Chapter III

In his final years, the writer of *"Amazing Grace,"* John Newton, suffered from dementia and from the loss of memory. Yet he confided, "I do remember two things: I am a great sinner, and Jesus is a Great Savior." When it comes to faith, those are the only things anyone needs to know. God's grace is sufficient and God's grace accepted is God's peace.

Once we trust in Christ as our Savior, we are new creations, and our past failings are just that, in the past. Any future mistakes are to be regarded as temporary setbacks: they do not define who we are. The Apostle Paul learned this lesson well. No matter how many times he was reviled, chased out of town, or stoned, he did not consider himself a failure. Rather, he looked to His Lord to determine the truth about who he was: a forgiven sinner commissioned to take the Gospel to the Gentiles Acts 22:10, 21. Difficulties may delay us in reaching our goals, but they aren't necessarily a dead end. Look at trials not as reasons to quit, but as opportunities that can assist us in reaching our goals. During our moments of defeat, God wants to teach us something that will help us succeed later on. We are sustained by such hope, even in our greatest crises.

Through the work of His Holy Spirit, our heavenly Father will give us the ability to stay on course. Do not give up. Draw near to the Lord, and allow His power to sustain you.

The bible assures us that there is *"no condemnation to those who are in Christ Jesus, who do not walk according to the flesh, but according to the Spirit"* Rom.8:1-11. We have been set *"free from the law of sin and death"* v.2. But the enemy of our soul tries to make us believe we are still dominated by sin. What shall we do then? Reflect on what Christ has done. *He died for our sins and declared an end to sin's control over us* v.3. He rose from the dead and gave us the Holy Spirit. Now we are empowered to live victoriously in Him because *"the Spirit of Him who raised Jesus from the dead dwells in us"* v.11. In Christ, we are set free. Experience true freedom; take every thought captive in obedience to Christ. *"Stand fast therefore in the liberty wherewith Christ hath made us free, and be not entangled again with the yoke of bondage"* Gal. 5:1.

The Holy Spirit lives inside us to be our helper in every situation. The night before His crucifixion, Jesus warned the disciples that He was about to depart. The news probably upset them, even though it wasn't the first time He'd spoken of His death. But the Lord offered His followers reassurance that He would send them another Helper. The Greek word for *"another"* implies that the new Helper would be like the previous one, in other words, a divine being with access to the Father. As promised, God's Spirit came to dwell in everyone who receives Jesus Christ as Savior Acts 2:1-4. Our Helper has a distinct role within the Trinity (He is the sustainer). The Father reigns over all; while the Son sits at His right hand interceding for believers. Meanwhile the Holy Spirit enables Christians to accomplish the work God has designed for each to do. The Father knew we couldn't follow Him without help, that was why Jesus told the disciples to remain in Jerusalem until after the arrival of the Holy Spirit. Whatever we are called to do in daily obedience or in lifelong vocation, our Helper offers direction. And when we are beset by tough times or temptations, God's Spirit provides strength and encouragement. The Holy Spirit is intimately involved in our life. He is more a part of us than our bones and blood. We are privileged to have a divine Helper guiding us on the path of God's will. AMEN!

Broken but Beautiful, Jeremiah 18:1-6 says the potter to the clay. In a similar way a broken life can be renewed when it is touched by God's love and grace. In the Old Testament, we read that when the Prophet Jeremiah watched a potter working, he noticed that if an object was marred (broken, cracked) the potter simply reshaped it. God explained that in His hands the people of ancient Israel were like clay, which He would shape as He saw best. We are never too badly broken for God to reshape us. He loves us in spite of our imperfections and past mistakes, and He desires to make us beautiful. Have thine own way, Lord! Have thine own way! Thou art the Potter; I am the clay; Mold me and make me after Thy will, while I am waiting, yielded and still. Have thine own way!!!

Walk worthy of the calling with which you were called; bearing one another in love, to keep the unity of the Spirit Ephes. 4:1-3. The frustrations of difficult people are what God has to endure with each of us every day; and He says some of you are just the sort of people; you have fatal flaws in your character. "All the hope and plans of others have again and again shipwrecked on your character just as your hopes and plans have shipwrecked on theirs." This self-awareness should motivate us to try to show the same patience and acceptance to others that God shows to us daily. In Ephesians, Paul exhorts us to arm ourselves relationally with all lowliness and gentleness, with longsuffering, bearing with one another in love. The one who is patient is better able to deal with a difficult person without becoming provoked to anger and retaliation. Instead, he or she is able to endure, exhibiting grace in spite of upsetting behavior. In dealing with difficult people we must see others as God sees us.

Prayer most Christians think that they need help in order to pray effectively. Well let me tell you, that you have a helper in prayer, The Spirit of God helps us with our weakness. We do not know how to pray as we should; but the Spirit Himself speaks to God for us, even begs God for us with deep feelings that words cannot explain. God can see what is in people's hearts. And He knows what is in the mind of the Spirit, because the Spirit speaks to God for His people in the way God wants <u>Romans 8:26-27.</u> Even the Apostle Paul said that he sometimes did not know how to petition the heavenly Father as he should. In the supernatural exchange between God and believers, the Holy Spirit acts as a vehicle for our communication, laying our needs and desires before the Father. We humans make our requests with a very limited knowledge of the future and an impaired sense of what is actually best for us. If all we know to ask is, "God, what is Your will?" Then the Spirit, who knows the Father's plans for us, tells Him of our need for understanding. Our Father doesn't hide His will from us. He desires to equip believers with all the information necessary for making the right decisions and for being continually conformed to the likeness of His Son. Just as the Spirit carries our needs to God, He also clarifies the Father's will to us. The Holy Spirit's divine nature prevents Him from going before God with a petition that is outside the Father's plan for our life. Instead, He intercedes to make the right request on our behalf. He also impresses upon us the need to adjust our desires. Therefore, we can pray in every situation, knowing the Holy Spirit is our Helper. But now if you don't have the Holy Spirit then; ask God in prayer to send the Holy Spirit in your life! You must be born again, and walking in obedience to the Lord, but you can't do it without the Holy Spirit! A prayerful life is very important!!!

Chapter III

The bible is God's revelation of truth, and it is intended for regular use by every believer. The Holy Spirit's indwelling presence is a necessity since He is the one who makes clear the meaning of the Word. He illuminates the mind of each person who genuinely seeks to know God. When we read, our Helper opens our understanding to the true meaning of the text so that we can grasp its significance. We never outgrow this need for Him. Even a mature believer with decades of experience meditating on Scripture requires as much revelation as a child who has just received Christ. Grasping a new revelation of truth from the Scriptures gets us excited and inspires us to apply what we have learned. Then, as we integrate one truth into our life, the Spirit of God reveals another in order to make us increasingly like our Savior. We can't expect to understand the bible if we refuse to obey its precepts. If we want the Holy Spirit to reveal biblical meaning, we must ask first for a revelation of our sin. When we have repented of the wrongdoing brought to mind by our Helper, our heart opens to His illumination.

Our hearts have to be clean to receive God's best for us. *Noah found grace in the eyes of the Lord* Genesis 6:8. We too have been shown God's grace through His Son Jesus' life, death, and resurrection. We have every reason to bring Him honor and stand strong for Him in our daily lives. He is always near, even abiding in us, so we never really stand alone. His *"ears are open to our cry"* Psalms 34:15. It's easy to stand with a crowd; it takes courage to stand alone. God wants to set you free from anything hindering your spiritual development.

Now with Pharaoh's army chasing after them; the Israelites were near panic. They did not see God's pathway for them (they saw no way out). But God parted the Red Sea and they walked through on dry land.

Years later, the psalm writer Asaph used this event as evidence of God's mighty power, *"Your road led through the sea, your pathway through the mighty waters, a pathway no one knew was there! You led Your people along that road like a flock of sheep, with Moses and Aaron as their shepherds"* Psalm 77:19-20. God can create roads where we see only obstacles. When the way ahead of us seems uncertain, it's good to remember what God has done in the past. He specializes in pathways in any circumstance, pathways that point us to His love and power.

Thank You God, for the miraculous ways You have worked in the past. Help me to never forget the pathways you have and can make for me when I need them; and Your power and faithfulness when I can see only trouble and difficulty. The God who created a way for our Salvation can certainly see us through our daily trials!!! Amen! *"Holy, Holy, Holy, Lord God Almighty, who was and is and is to come!"* Revelations 4:8. Like the four creatures, we were designed to glorify God. Our lives will never be boring if we're focusing our attention on Him fulfilling that purpose. *Holy, Holy, Holy! Merciful and mighty! God in three Persons blessed Trinity!!!* A heart in tune with God can't help but to sing His praise.

There are some of you out there that are so insecure that even you don't know it. To begin with, insecure people have difficulty establishing good, lasting relationships. They simply cannot see how they could add value to anyone else's life. This is a tragic loss, because every one of us needs deep and meaningful friendships to help us grow. Also men and women with insecurity are often seen as prideful or snobbish. Lack of confidence may cause them to withdraw from others, which can easily be mistaken for an act of arrogance. They simply don't want to be around others. What's more, insecurity frequently leads to indecisiveness and fear. People can be so consumed with self-doubt that they can't make any decision at all. They wonder what if I make a mistake. So what if you do; if you don't try you won't succeed. Don't be afraid of trying. Even if you don't succeed, you can at least rest in knowing that you did your best, and that's anything you try Marriage, friendships anything. After a while, insecure people typically become angry. When they go so long feeling so poorly about themselves, they start to resent the success and happiness of others. Can you see how something as subtle as a lack of confidence can have a debilitating effect on one's life and everyone around you? Don't let such devastation affect your relationships. Pray for ability to recognize areas of self-doubt, and then take a step toward freedom today, asks the Lord to help heal your insecurities. Amen! *"Let this mind be in you, which is also in Christ Jesus"* Phil. 2:5. *"And the peace of God, which passes all understanding, shall keep your hearts and mind through Christ Jesus"* Phil. 4:7. God did not make a mistake when He made you!

This is what Jesus calls us to do, to be obedient to the Word of God Simply. *"You shall love the Lord your God with all your heart, with all your soul, with all your mind, and with all your strength.' This is the first commandment. And the second is like the first: 'You shall love your neighbor as yourself.' There is no other commandment greater than these"* Mark 12:30-31.

Faith is Christ is simple and His burden is light. I Thank you Lord for loving me; and saving me. God's love in our heart gives us a heart for Him and others.

The Apostle Paul reminded Timothy to *"be strong in the grace that is in Christ Jesus. And the things you have heard me say in the presence of many witnesses entrust to reliable men who will also be qualified to teach others"* 2 Timothy 2:1-2. When we remember that our strength is a result of God's grace, that keeps us humble, then in humility we pass on God's truth by being an example that encourages and inspires others to follow. Jesus Himself is our example of servant hood. He gave His very life for us! Lord Jesus, I know little about humility, show me and teach me as I read about Your example in Your Word. Give me the grace to humble myself and serve others. Humility is the result of knowing the One true God and knowing yourself.

You know you can compare my dream about JayQuan to another young man name Joseph. Joseph was 17 and JayQuan was 18 and they knew at a young age that God loved and favored them; they tried everything that they could to do God's will in their lives. First they demonstrated a servant spirit early in life. They never acted out against those in authority over them. They always went out of their way to serve others. Most teen are prone to selfishness, but they were taught from an early age that a real man is a servant to others. Second they realized at a young age that God was controlling their lives no matter what it may look like on the outside (trials). They were convinced that there was a plan for their lives and that somehow, sometime, God would reveal what it was. Whether you are 17, 18 or 99, it is never too late to learn the art of service or to recognize God's perfect plan. Even better, it's never too late to help someone else discover these things.

One thing they did take with them is their faith in God. Life is like that at times for every one of us. Sudden changes in health or finances, the unexpected death of a loved one, or abandonment by a good friend can bring us into a dark season. We do not understand why the Lord has allowed the trial or let the pain continue. Even in a foreign state for JayQuan and a foreign country for Joseph, they experienced the blessing of God's presence. One of the keys to walking through dark valleys, those times when life seems to be crumbling and the future's looking grim is to embrace the reality of the Lord's presence with us. At the moment of salvation, the Holy Spirit comes to live permanently within the new Christian and seals him or her as belonging to God forever! Amen! Take a few minutes each day and reflect on Jesus' promise to be with us always Matt.28:20. The result will be that this truth becomes planted deep within your soul to sustain you in hard times.

First, the Lord is a faithful companion who uses our troubles to prepare us for His work. Second, when the Lord accomplishes His purposed, the difficulty will end, and we become stronger in the Lord. Remember, even Jesus suffered in order to fulfill God's redemptive purpose Matt.16:21. We will never suffer as much as Jesus did for us.

For you are a chosen generation, a royal priesthood, a Holy Nation, a peculiar people; that you should show forth the praises of Him who has called you out of darkness into His marvelous light 1 Peter 2:9.

We hurt others when our actions are not Christ like. We forget sometimes that people struggling with faith, in their lives, are watching Christians with expectation. They hope to see less anger and more mercy, less judgment and more compassion, less criticism and more encouragement. Jesus and Peter told us to live good lives so God is given the glory Matt. 5:16; 1 Peter 2:12. May our action and reactions point to those around us to our Loving Father! In our life for Christ we accomplish nothing without the Spirit! May others see less of me and more of Jesus!

A time of rejoicing, because we have hope! "He is not here; for He is risen, as He said Matt. 28:6. *Because Jesus had come back to life, death had been conquered! Jesus reminded His followers just a few days before His death: "Because I live, you will live also"* John 14:19. Thank You, Lord, for comfort and hope. What would we do without You? Your death, burial and resurrection provide all we need for this life and the next. Because He lives, I can face tomorrow, because He lives all fear is lose, because I know who hold the future and life is worth the living just because He lives!! Hallelujah!!!! Amen!

We are ambassadors for Christ: 2Corin. 5:20. Just as God sent Christ to reconcile us to Himself; we now have the ministry of reconciliation. Our message is that all can be redeemed in Christ because God made Him who knew no sin to be sin for us, that we might become the righteousness of God in Him. Let's take our role seriously. Wherever God places us in the world, He can use us as walking billboards of reconciliation for Christ Jesus.

Adversity can be painful, but the Lord uses it to further His purposes and equip us for His plan. Bitterness is a toxin that we prepare for someone else but then drink ourselves. It is a concentrated dose of emotional poison, often one that we carefully nurture and grow over the course of years. When we react to someone's wrongdoing by withdrawing and giving free reign to daydreams of retribution and ill-will, we are slowly poisoning our own hearts and minds. I know this because if happen to me for years I still couldn't forgive myself for the things I allowed to happen to me. Ask God to reveal any signs of poison in your system. Then ask Him to help you administer a dose of the antidote: FORGIVENESS!

Let me tell you, you don't want to let this continue, because it causes all kinds of illnesses. Hebrews 12:15 says that bitterness is a root that grows over years. Can you see how this image "root" can stop your spiritual growth? Perhaps you have a root of bitterness don't feed it, don't let it grow. A root of bitterness will never produce healthy fruit; when the root is harmful, it is senseless to expect anything other than bad fruit. Remember there is a remedy to this problem. All it takes to kill a weed is to unearth and dispose of the root. Pull the source of your resentment out of its hiding place. Expose it and give it to God, who knows how to cultivate the heart.

Like a loving father, God wants His family united. We cannot accomplish what God has for us to do if we refuse to be reconciled with one another. In His most impassioned prayer, on the night before He was crucified, Jesus pleaded with God to unite His followers: *"That they all may be one, as You, Father, are in Me, and I in You; that they also may be one in Us"* John 17:21. Singing Illustrates unity as we agree on the lyrics, chords, and rhythms; singing can also promote unity as it binds us together in peace, proclaims God's power through praise, and demonstrates God's glory to the world. Singing God's praises will never go out of style. Amen!

"Bear with one another in love, endeavoring to keep the unity of the Spirit in the bond of peace" Ephesians 4:2-3.

Surely I am coming quickly! Revelation 22:20. Here we all wait for the Lord to come quickly, are you still waiting? Look to the Lord and be of good courage He will appear as He said He would. For the return we still wait; watch and wait. Waiting tries our faith and so we wait in hope. Amen!

So it is with us when God asks us to follow Him. He wants to lead us to a place of closer fellowship with Himself. His Word assures us that He is loving and faithful in leading those who humbly follow Him. In fellowship sweet we will sit at His feet, or we'll walk by His side in the way; what He says we will do, where He sends we will go; never fear, only trust and obey for there no other way but to love the Lord and trust and obey! God ask His children to follow Him and keep standing on His promises.

Preparation for greater service; in Luke 17:5, the apostles asked Christ to increase their faith. The Lord told them that if they had faith as small as a mustard seed, they could do great things. God does not enlarge our faith instantly. He begins with what little we have and proceeds to grow it. Take 1Kings 17:1-24. God is preparing Elijah for greater things; each act of believing God and the steps of obedience resulted in increased opportunities for Elijah to serve the Lord and others. Raising the dead may seem like the height of Elijah's ministry, but it was to be followed by an even greater opportunity to influence an entire nation for God. Elijah was about to face the biggest spiritual battle of his life! 1Kings 18; all his previous demonstrations of faith and obedience were the Lord's way of preparing Him. God wants each of us to be influential in His Kingdom. He knows which faith challenges to present so that we can be entrusted with even greater tasks. The Lord will provide occasions for you to believe Him and respond in obedience, we call them "problems." Begin to look at each difficulty as an opportunity designed by God specifically for the purpose of increasing your faith so He can do great things in and through you! Amen!

Think of faith and obedience as travel companions; heading in the same destination, namely to please and glorify the Lord. You cannot have one without the other. They grow simultaneously as they are practiced but will wither if neglected. Elijah had both of these qualities. He believed God and always responded in obedience. When told by the Lord to show himself to King Ahab, Elijah didn't permit fear to stop Him. He had learned through experience that the Father was faithful and trustworthy.

Fear short-circuits faith when we begin to doubt that God's way is really best. If we allow worry to gain a foothold in our minds, (like Adam & Eve) we'll respond by refusing to do what the Lord says, which is disobedience, the results can be devastating, and by rejecting the way of faith and obedience, we're actually choosing the path of unbelief and sin. Satan loves our fear and disobedience because they hinder the journey that God has designed for us. We can't believe the Lord for great things in one area of our life if we are allowing sin to creep in, in another. Where's the victory we talk about, we have to believe God He knows best! Examine yourself in the walk of faith. Where have you compromised by allowing sin a foothold? Are you resisting anything God says in His Word? Great faith begins with small steps. When you choose to follow God's Word and ever-increasing cycle of faith and obedience will begin. Don't let fear or sin rob you of the great adventure God's planned for your life!

Now the risk of obeying God is overflow. God is more than enough for you. Trust and obey for there's no other way. God will never instruct us to do anything unless He has a specific, sovereign purpose for it Jeremiah 29:11. What we have yet to learn is that apart from the supernatural involvement of Almighty God, every bit of self-effort is in vain. You will never understand the kind of reward you will receive from God when you are obedient. The thing that you sought and desire most of all God gave, because of obedience, overflow. The difference is that it was in God's time and God's way. Trust Him He knows what's best for you and me. You'll never know the reward until you're willing to take the risk, and the greater the risk, the greater the reward.

The bible is a guidebook mapping the route to our eternal home. But travelers must read and follow the directions. Some people claim they will get to heaven because of their morality, their religious observances, or even their belief that God exists. But those paths lead to death. Let me tell you the devil believes God exists. The only road that leads to the Lord's eternal home *is faith in Jesus Christ* John 14:6. First you must believe you are a sinner: Everyone has done wrong Isa.53:6; Rom. 3:23. But only someone under the convicting power of the Holy Spirit recognizes that sin is what separates us from our Holy God. Second, Jesus is perfect: Christ's sinless sacrifice on the cross is what brought us back into the foal. Our Savior paid all past, present, and future sin debt. Hallelujah!! Amen! Three you must realized that you need Jesus: You must believe that Jesus is who He says He is! Then you must repent and turn away from old sins. Then you are given a brand-new nature; and is welcomed into God's family 2Corin.5:17; John1:12.

If you stay the course: redemption Rom.3:24, *eternal life* John 3:15, and a great adventure walking with Jesus. Trust in the Savior, and thank Him for His mercy and grace. Amen!

Our foundation is Jesus Christ! *The Lord Jesus came to our world from heaven* John 3:13. When He went back into heaven after His death and resurrection, He left followers who became the *"living temple"* of God, of which He is the foundation. For no other foundation can anyone lay than that which is laid, which is Jesus Christ 1Corin. 3:11. The Spiritual Church is founded on the ultimate heavenly foundation, Christ Jesus Isa.28:16; 1Corin.10:3-4. I Paul have planted, Apollos watered; but God gave the increase 1Corin.3:6! Praise God that because of what Jesus has done our Salvation is secure.

Christ the Solid Rock is our sure hope.

This can happen in our walk of faith in Christ, when our commitment to God seems too much to bear. But the Lord has an encouraging word for us when our confidence wavers. This word is for the people who have struggled all these years, God will reward you if you have patience and confidence and continue to press on and never turn back Hebrews 10:35-39. Our confidence is not in ourselves but in Jesus and His promise to return at just the right time. It is God's power that enables us to continue in our journey of faith. Trusting God's faithfulness in past years stirs up our confidence in Him today and forever! Amen!

In today's world we still try to as they say, "past the buck" never taking responsibility for our sin we just like Adam and Eve try to cover it up. Instead of acknowledging and confessing sin, we frequently look for a quick fix to the situation. When sin breaks our fellowship with the Lord, we avoid prayer and time in the Scriptures because we're struggling with sin and feeling guilty. So we always put the blame on other people. Adam blamed Eve and God, Eve blamed the serpent, and no one took responsibility for their actions. Our sin is never bad enough to keep God away; God still calls to us and asks, *"Where are you?"* Genesis 3:9. He knows what we have done and why, but He questions us so that we can come to realize our desperate need for Him. Never let guilt or shame keep you from the Lord. He seeks those who have made a mess of their life and speaks to them through His Word, His Spirit, and His people. Forgiveness and a restored relationship await all who are willing to listen, confess, and repent.

Unto the upright there arises light in the darkness; He is gracious, and full of compassion Ps.112:4. Paul says in 1Corin.13 that if we don't have love, our voices clang on people's ears and our faith means nothing. And the Apostle John says that if we have material possessions and see others in need and take action, that's evidence that God's love is abiding in us 1John 3:16. The One True God desires; that we deal *"graciously"* Ps.112:5 with those in need; for His heart is gracious toward us. Kindness is Christianity with its working clothes on! Amen!

Praying effectively isn't something we naturally know how to do, for most Christians, it must be learned. In fact, one of the disciples who walked with Jesus asked for help in this area Luke 11:1. So often we hear requests to bless, protect, and provide for a person. These are fine to ask of the Lord, there is another, more powerful way to pray: When we use Scripture to speak to the Heavenly Father, our conversation contains

His own divine authority. The Apostle Paul says: It shows us the specific requests he brought before God concerning the church. Paul prayed that the Christians would understand God's plan for their lives. Also conduct themselves in a manner worthy of Christ and pleasing to Him, and their true spiritual identity. A follower of Jesus is evident to other people because of lifestyle and spiritual fruit Gal. 5:22-23. One of the greatest gifts we can give is to lift a person in prayer. And there is no more powerful way to do this than to speak Scripture on his or her behalf. Amen! Also Paul prayed may they bear fruit in every work; and to grow in the knowledge of God by studying His word more each day, and listening to sermons, and an understanding of the heart concerning the Lord; and also, to be strengthened according to His Power. Also please walk in gratitude for what the Lord has done for you.

In the busyness of today's world, prayer often gets squeezed out of our schedules. But communion with the Lord is vital to a healthy, vibrant relationship with Him. Remember that lifting our loved ones before God's throne is far more important than many tasks which seem more pressing.

"You are the light of the world. A city that is set on a hill cannot be hid. "Let your light so shine before men, that they may see your good works, and glorify your Father which is in Heaven" Matt. 5:14,16. Small acts of kindness and love, can keep the darkness at bay. That's what Jesus teaches us as well; Warning us that we would live in dark times. He reminded us that because of Him we are the light of the world, and that our good deeds would be the power against the darkness for the glory of God. There is one force that the darkness cannot conquer, the force of loving acts of kindness done in Jesus' name. It is God's people

who turn the other cheek, go the extra mile, and forgive and even love their enemies who oppose them who have the power to turn the tide against evil. So look for the privileged opportunity to perform acts of kindness today to bring the light of Christ to others. Always treat others the way you would want to be treated. Don't give the devil a foothold, love one another.

"Oh give thanks unto the Lord; for He is good! Because His mercy endures forever" Ps.118:1,8. *"It is better to put confidence in the Lord than to put confidence in man and princes."* Never forget the grace of God! *"Mercy"* means *"Steadfast Love."* It refers to God's faithfulness to us. He has promised to be present always to care for His children. By remembering specific ways God has provided for us in the past, we can change our perspective for the better. God's steadfast love endures forever! You should always remember God's provisions for yesterday give hope and strength for today.

In Matthew 28:16-20; Jesus mentions discipleship, baptism, and teaching. We all agree that discipleship and teaching are essential to growing in faith; however, some Christians postpone or ignore the commandment to be baptized. The will of God is that every person who receives salvation participates in the biblically mandated practice. Jesus Himself commanded every person who receives salvation should be baptized. Once Jesus delivered this charge to His followers, baptism was no longer optional. Scripture contains several examples of new Christians who submitted in obedience immediately after salvation, Paul and Silas instructed their Jailer to receive Christ and be baptized Acts 16:27-33. And also, Phillip took the Ethiopian eunuch right into the water after hearing his confession of faith Acts8:36-38. Too many believers today procrastinate because they do not perceive baptism as a command or recognize delay as rebellion. We claim *God as our Father and Jesus Christ as Savior,* and we acknowledge that *the Holy Spirit* lives in us. The willingness to humble ourselves in this way honors *God as Lord* of our life. Baptism by immersion also symbolizes the transforming power of salvation. We are buried to demonstrate we have died to old habits; we are raised to show we now walk in newness of life Romans 6:4. This is known has **"God's Great Commission."**

Jesus after His Resurrection came to His disciples and ask them to wait a little longer for Him to set up Kingdom on earth. But they were to do more than wait. Jesus told His followers that they were to *"be witness to Him in Jerusalem and in all Judea and Samaria, and to the ends of the earth"* Acts 1:8. And He gave them the Holy Spirit to empower them to do this. We still wait for Jesus' return. And while we wait, it's our delight, in the Holy Spirit's power, to tell and show others who He is, what He has done for all of us through His death and resurrection, and that He has promised to return! Amen! Wait and Witness till Jesus return! Hallelujah!!! Go tell everybody about Jesus!!

Your word is a lamp to my feet and a light to my path Ps.119:105. That's what happens when we seek the Lord word day by day with an open heart and a willing spirit. With God as your navigator, you're headed in the right direction, Spiritual navigation.

Spiritual combat is going on all the time. It is important for believers to be aware of this conflict in order to battle sin effectively and live in a manner pleasing to God. The struggle exists in three areas. **First,** we have as internal enemy: But the Holy Spirit can draw us and move our thoughts towards the Lord. However, even after salvation, we have the capacity to do wrong as long as we remain in the carnal body. Scripture cites evidence of the old *"flesh"* patterns at work within us, patterns such as immorality, impurity, jealousy, and outbursts of anger Galatians 5:19-20. That's not of God that's disobedience. **Second,** we have an external enemy: the ungodly beliefs, attitudes, and philosophies all around us. 1John 2:15 warns, *"If anyone loves the world, the love of the Father is not in him or her."* As believers n Jesus, we should be salt and light to the world around us without allowing its ways to influence our thoughts or behavior. **Third,** there's an infernal enemy, and his name is Satan. His desire is to dishonor God and to gain victory over the Lord's Kingdom. We know from Scripture that this will not happen, we have already won the war, Jesus overcame the devil, but the conflict will continually rage on until the final days mentioned on Revelation, **the Last Days, which is God's day of reckoning!** Be aware of these three enemies. You wouldn't sleep in the midst of a raging war, and neither should you live without awareness in the daily spiritual battle. Ephesians 6:10-13 says: *"Finally, my brethren, be strong in the Lord, and in the power of His might. Put on the whole armor of God that we may be able to stand against the wiles of the devil. For we wrestle not against flesh and blood, but against principalities, against powers, against the rulers of darkness of this world, against spiritual wickedness in high places. Wherefore take unto you the* **Whole Armor of God,** *that you may be able to withstand in the evil day, and having to done all stand."* Arm yourself with God's Word, and seek His protection and wisdom.

Sometimes people frequently face situations bigger than they can handle. Sometimes its temporary despair brought on by fatigue, as in Elijah's case. He had been part of a great victory over the prophets of

Chapter III

Baal 1Kings18:20, but then he feared for his life and ran into the wilderness 19:1-3. But often, it's more than despair and it's more than temporary. That's why it is imperative that we talk about depression openly and compassionately. God offers His presence to us in life's darkest moments, which enables us, in turn, to be His presence to the hurting. Crying out for help, from others and from God, *may be the strongest moment of our lives. Father, grant us the candor to admit to each other that sometimes life overwhelms us. And grant us the courage to help others find help, and to seek it when we need it. Hope comes with help from God and others.*

The divinity of Jesus Christ is one of the most controversial issues facing every human being; it is also the most critical. Our faith hangs in the balance on this question. There are many people who say they believe in Jesus and in God, but do not think that Jesus is God. They believe many good things about Him, however. They accept Him as a teacher. They believe that He was a healer. They revere Him as a philosopher, revolutionary, and social reformer. And yet, they cannot, or rather will not, accept Him as Lord. I want to be very clear about this matter. You can believe all of these wonderful things about Jesus. You can go so far as to sing praises to Him as a prophet sent by almighty God. But if you do not accept that He is who He says He is, one with God, The Savior who died for your sins, then you do not know Him at all. Now, you may have heard people argue that Jesus Himself never actually claimed to be God. This is not true. Time and again in the Gospels, Jesus places Himself on equal footing with the Father and the Holy Spirit John 10:30; 14:6-14. The truth is if Jesus was not truly God's Son, then He was a lunatic or a liar. Not so He was as He said you have seen me so you have seen the Father. If you're the least bit uncertain about this eternal question, don't let another minute pass before taking steps to figure out the answer. Take the time to examine the Gospels. Talk to your pastor or believing friends. Settle for yourself the life changing question, "Was Jesus Christ really God?" Because in the end when they say every knee shall bow and every tongue confess that Jesus Christ is Lord, you don't want to be on the wrong side of that question! Amen!

Is Jesus your Lord and Savior? Too many He is much more. Jesus did something for us that had never been done before: He enabled us to see the Father in a new way. In Col. 1:15: Paul explains that Jesus is the *"Image of the invisible God."* No one has ever gazed upon the face of the Almighty. In the Old Testament, some people found themselves in His presence, but they were never able to look fully upon His glory. For example, even the great Prophet Moses, who conversed with God as one would with a friend, couldn't look directly at Him. At best, he had the opportunity to get a glimpse of "God's back" as the Lord passed by, but not His face Colossians 1:18-23. However, Jesus came to bridge the gap between the Father's pure, holy glory and mankind's sinful nature. As God's *"image,"* Jesus is the exact, flawless replica, the perfect reflection of His Father and ours. Therefore, Jesus could say, *"He who has seen Me has seen the Father"* John 14:9. How do we know what the Heavenly Father is like? By knowing Jesus! He is the only full expression and explanation of God. Ask the Father today to reveal His Son to you in a fresh way. He is the great I AM!!

Jesus is the very picture of Humility; from washing the disciple's feet, to dying on the cross for everyone who excepts Him John 13:1-11. God resists the proud, but gives grace to the humble James 4:6. In Jesus washing the disciple's feet symbolized, Christ's cleaning, a cleansing that will never be realized unless we are willing to be humble before the Savior! We receive God's grace when we acknowledge the greatness of God; who Humbled Himself at the cross!!! Philippians 2:5-11. *"The most powerful position on earth is kneeling before the Lord of the Universe!"*

Jesus offers us forgiveness of sin; peace with God and presence of the Holy Spirit. In return, all He asks is that we do good Gal. 6:10, *forgive as we've been forgiven* Luke 6:37, *and love others as He loves us* John 13:34. The beauty of Jesus' convenient with us is that even though we fail to live up to our end of the terms, we still receive the blessings, (but we need to repent). As we have opportunity, let us do good to all. God is looking for strong warriors.

Every need we will experience in life is already met in Christ Jesus. By His power, God has prepared blessings to fill each of our needs in His perfect timing. We think that we must have certain things in a particular time frame, (which with most people it is the now frame), but the Lord knows better. Sometimes there is a need in our life, whether it is physical, spiritual, relational, emotional, or financial, persist because the Lord is trying to get our attention. He wants us to focus on Him so that He can correct our thinking. He knows we cannot enjoy blessing until He has been allowed to work in our life. Like a fruit tree, we must be pruned; sometimes the cutting back hurts, but it is always followed by a more bountiful harvest. He wants His children to come with boldness and confidence, anticipating the blessings He longs to give! God knows what's best and is intently interested in our well being. While He does not promise ease, God is certainly steadfast in proving us spiritual comfort and meeting our every need.

Galatians 5:1 tells us *"Christ has truly set us free, and do not be entangled by the yoke of bondage again."* The reason we can know genuine freedom is that Jesus *"has granted to us everything pertaining to life and godliness, through the true knowledge of Him who called us"* 2 Peter 1:3. God says that you and I have been granted everything we will ever need to live a triumphant Christian life. The Lord's glorious provision, however, begins only after we trust Christ for salvation. We have to take the plunge of faith before His divine power is released into our life. Once we've taken the step of believing in Jesus, all things are available, including courage, forgiveness, vision, wisdom, and a deepening trust in God!

Many people pass it by with hardly an acknowledgement. Others look and wonder what needs to happen for it to become a reality in their life. As with all of God's promises, you must accept it before you can act upon it. And just because you recognize and accept the promise as yours is one thing, applying it in your daily life can be quite another matter. Ultimately, the promise is realized by the full experiential knowledge of Jesus as we hunger and thirst for the Living Water Jesus supplies.

Sometimes our fears can lead to inaction. We worry so much about protecting ourselves that we fail to simply step up. When King Asa learned that the Lord wanted him to remove the idols from Israel, he took courage 2 Chron. 15:8, 15. He could have had a rebellion on his hands for doing this. But he stepped up, and as a result the nation rejoiced. If facing a spiritual challenge, the Lord will help you step out on faith and courage and trust Him for the outcome. Have no fear trust in Jesus, He will see you through! Amen!

When we were yet dead in our sins, Jesus Christ gave His life to come to our aid. We were the ones He came to rescue. He came down from heaven above and pulled us to safety. He did this by taking the punishment for all of our wrongdoing as he died on the cross 1Peter 2:24 and 3 days later was resurrected. The bible says, *"By this we know love, because Jesus laid down His life for us"* 1 John 3:16. Jesus' sacrificial love for us now inspires us to show genuine love in deed and in truth 1 John3:18 to others with whom we have relationships. And this is His Commandment; That we should believe on the name of his Son Jesus Christ, and love one another, as He gave us commandment 1 John 3:23.

If we overlook Jesus' ultimate sacrifice on our behalf, we'll fail to see and experience His love. Today, consider the connection between His sacrifice and His love for you. He has come to rescue you, reach out for His hand! Jesus laid down His life to show His love for us!! Hallelujah!! Amen!!!

The Ultimate Sacrifice!!!

Trust in the Lord with all your heart and lean not unto your own understanding and in all your ways acknowledge Him and He will direct your paths Proverbs 3:5-6. Stay with me, and join in on the study of learning who God is, in my next Book!